7

An Englishman's
Peace and War

An Englishman's Peace and War

NEIL BOYD

ERRATA

Two mis-spellings occur in the
caption to the photograph
on page 160.
In line two for Durch read Dutch
In line three for hapanese read Japanese.

The Pentland Press
Edinburgh – Cambridge – Durham – USA

© Neil Boyd, 1994

First published in 1994
by The Pentland Press Ltd
1 Hutton Close
South Church
Bishop Auckland
Durham

British Library
Cataloguing-in-Publication Data

A catalogue record for this book
is available from the British Library

ISBN 1-85821-215-4

Typeset by Carnegie Publishing Ltd., 18 Maynard St., Preston
Printed and bound in Great Britain by Bookcraft (Bath) Ltd.

CONTENTS

LIST OF ILLUSTRATIONS

AUTHOR'S NOTE

THE WEIGHT OF THE RESPONSIBILITY to my dead comrades seems to be too much for me as I give my testimony to the uselessness of many things which are most prized. It is my consciousness of this which has finally led me to set down my own experiences in the Second World War.

Encouraged by a caring family, writing these memoirs has involved reliving my story as it unfolds an indelible sequence of events.

An undercurrent of a strange insistence to 'love your enemies' has religious connotations.

Not all has been told and some names have been deliberately withheld, but there are no fictitious persons and no fictitious events in this account.

All sketches and illustrations are my own work.

This is a true story exactly as it happened.

To the memory of all my dead comrades. When in difficulties in the field there was none more resourceful than the British 'Tommy', who endured and suffered for the freedom of mankind.

Constrained to revisit camps in the Far East which held me, and also Dachau in Germany, I have paid my respects to the dead.

FOREWORD

MAINLY an account of my own experiences during the
Second World War, this book begins with a summary of
my life in the Army which I joined as a Cavalryman in
September 1934.

Five years later, when war was declared in September 1939, a
whole catastrophic experience engulfed me, prohibiting any
further possibility of leading a normal life.

I was one of the original Desert Rats with the Royal
Armoured Corps. We were battle weary and ill-equipped during
and after the desert campaign, when an onerous decision sent a
small force to a one-sided conflict.

Sent under a foreign flag to Sumatra via Ceylon (now Sri
Lanka) with no Naval protection on the high seas, to meet
jungle-trained Japanese, our highly seasoned troops were outnumbered by at least a thousand to one.

Never since Genghis Khan, the great Mongol conqueror, had
such terrible hordes swept through Asia unopposed.

Separated from my unit when sent out on a Special Mission
(which was fulfilled) the treachery of two British Officers
brought about my ultimate capture.

My story reveals the untenable conditions endured in POW
camps uncharted, and the tyranny of the Japanese authority to
which I was subjected.

Deluged by a multitude of flat yellow faces, the only route to escape was an estimated seven hundred miles across the sea of Japan to Vladivostock in the USSR, a physical impossibility when one was disease-ridden and emaciated.

Learning to detach my conscious being from my physically tormented body I was consequently supported throughout by a spiritual strength hitherto unknown to me. Improbabilities of an incomprehensible nature intervened in various guises on several occasions to snatch me from certain death.

Whatever preconceptions there may be, my experiences were solid and incontrovertible.

Becoming a victim of the atomic bomb of Hiroshima, subsequent official incompetence fell upon my unprotected shoulders, and I was subjected to a journey half-way round the world with an open wound.

With restoration to freedom, the harvest was a travesty of justice.

PORTS OF CALL
1942 -45

COLOMBO
CEYLON
Palembang Sumatra
BATAVIA. JAVA
now called DJAKARTA
JOKJKARTA. JAVA

SINGAPORE

BANGKOK
Siam
FORMOSA
now Taiwan
OKINAWA
small island
south of Nippon

JAPAN
KYUSHU
HONSHU or
NIPPON
KURE
HIROSHIMA
KOBE
WAKAYAMA
OKINAWA
PHILIPPINE
ISLANDS
MANILA
CORREGIDOR
HAWAIIAN ISLANDS
HONOLULU
AMERICA
SAN FRANCISCO
WASHINGTON
STATE
TACOMA
SEATTLE

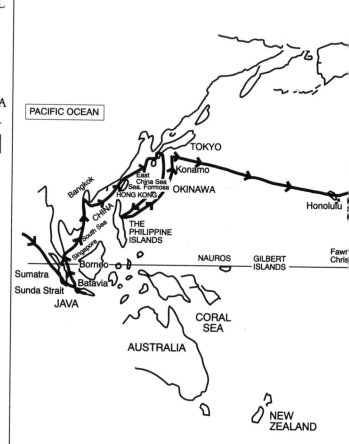

PACIFIC OCEAN

TOKYO

Konamo

Bangkok

East
China Sea
Sea. Formosa
HONG KONG

OKINAWA

Honolulu

CHINA

South Sea

THE
PHILIPPINE
ISLANDS

NAUROS

GILBERT
ISLANDS

Fawr
Chris

Singapore

Borneo

Sumatra

Batavia

Sunda Strait

JAVA

CORAL
SEA

AUSTRALIA

NEW
ZEALAND

*The above map is incomplete in that
it does not show the myriad of
small islands in the Pacific Ocean.
It is only meant to show my route
to Nippon and across the Pacific.*

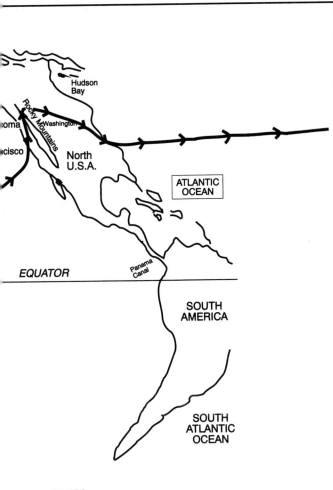

CANADA
OVER THE
ROCKY
MOUNTAINS
Mt. Edithcavell
Nat. Park
11,033 ft.
British Columbia
then
overland to
Saskatchewan
PRINCE ALBERT
FORT WILLIAM
Lake Superior
U.S.A.
DETROIT
LAKE CLAIR
LONG ISLAND
NEW YORK
then
across the
Atlantic
to
Southampton

SHIPS
1. A NORWEGIAN SHIP Name printed out
2. SINGAPORE MARU Japanese
3. U.S.S. SANCTUARY U.S.A.
4. MARINE SHARK U.S.A.
5. QUEEN MARY British

PART ONE

EARLY DAYS IN KHAKI

M Y TIME goes back to the old Cavalry recruit days at Tidworth and Aldershot in the 1930s, when many times I felt the cane of the rough-riding Sergeant-Major across my backside to speed my vaulting into the saddle.

In the years ahead my greatest nostalgia sprang from involvement with the horses. The trumpet-call, 'Water your horses and give them some corn,' was the beginning of each day's activity.

At 5.30 a.m., steeped with the smell of linseed, oats and hay, the horses were watered and fed before being taken out and exercised. Then 'mucking out' with one fork between a dozen men sharpened our appetite for the hearty breakfast to which we returned before grooming our charges, then going on to gymnasium exercise.

Studying for my Army First to qualify for promotion meant attending school in the early afternoons, which was followed by PT and drill before cleaning the harness with Kiwi, saddle-soap and Meppo polish. Inspection was held and charges made against slip-shod work, if any.

We were paraded for Guard Duty about 6 p.m. The cleanest man on parade was dismissed – all borrowed kit of course – with Blanco'd braces, boned boots, burnished swords and boot hobnails; Blanco'd white chaps inside the leg.

Shrill words of command and 'The Last Post' sounded at 10 p.m. Long nights followed with restless horses and the novelty of the regimental mascot – our donkey – who always took refuge behind a big stallion in a loose horse box.

The Orderly Officer for the night carried out impromptu visits and, irrespective of the hour, speedy compliance to disciplined orders averted swift retribution.

To our dismay our equine world was suddenly shattered when big German Prussians came to buy our lovely horses, except the Colonel's white charger.

We were to be mechanized.

New to mechanization I drove sedately along the Grand Trunk Road at Tidworth where, to keep a straight course on a heavily armoured tracked vehicle, constant adjustment of two tillers was necessary. On one occasion I pulled the right tiller and, unaware that the tracks were going faster than the engine (which forced the tank-steering into reverse), turned left and crashed into the Hussars' tailoring shop directly opposite the driveway to the Hussars Officers' Mess (the main arterial road used by all the Regiments).

With a wrecked tank I faced a serious charge, and was invited to comment. 'Now I know why Captains go down with their ships,' promptly got me marched out. Later I was relegated to Austin Sevens for a considerable time.

The entrance road of the accident was used by the Garrison when on church parades, and my Regiment, the 3rd King's Own Hussars, always went first as it marched at the slower pace of 120 steps to the minute, requiring a head start over the other Regiments. There was always a meticulous inspection by the Colonel, but I discovered that volunteering to sing in the choir (in civilian clothes) enabled me to deviate to a different route passing the barracks of the Argyll and Sutherland Highlanders.

When on full-dress parade it amused me to see the CO inspecting the Regiment with a mirror on a long cane held beneath the kilt to ensure everyone was correctly undressed.

Seconded to the Grenadier Guards at Chelsea Barracks for cadre classes on small-arms I sat in the guard room watching the Guardsmen checking out. Polished and immaculately turned out, they were revolved before a long mirror with one in three being sent back with harsh commands. High standards were always enforced by the Regiment. Incentive for the cleanest man on parade was to wear the white Sam Browne and act as the Colonel's Orderly for the next day.

Intensive training on the 'Tomson' sub-machine gun (Tommy Gun) did not prevent me becoming involved with the lovely Argentine polo ponies billeted in civilian stables. I took some of them to Hurlingham. The team to be played was Captained by Hollywood film director, Daryl Zannuck (he discovered Betty Grable who I was to meet in 1945).

A few days later such activities were cancelled for the Coronation of King George VI and the glamour of our Hussar uniform: mail-chain; tunics of blue with gold trappings; busbies; and highly-polished rough-riding knee boots with spurs.

Although I did not accompany my Regiment to Aldershot my deployment to Fleet in Hampshire was a happy time. Later I rejoined my colleagues at Jellalabad Barracks in Tidworth, where in 1938 the Queen (now Queen Mother) visited us. She was a gracious lady and had the troops fall out to mix informally with them. Enquiring about the welfare of ourselves and families, she shared our sadness at the loss of our long-nosed friends.

With war imminent we moved to Cambridgeshire on manoeuvres where I sped along in my little Austin Seven with a blue triangular wooden-board on the bonnet, supposed to represent a tank.

Returning to Salisbury Plain, practice with live ammunition in a cornfield incurred several casualties. Further training was received at the armoured school of the Royal Regiment of Tanks at Bovington, Dorset. Here I was fortunate to meet ex-Colonel Lawrence (of Arabia) but shocked to hear of his death the next day in a motorcycle accident.

Then came the rains, with straw palliasses in our bell-tents floating remarkably like rubber dinghies as the duckboards disappeared into the mire. It was a struggle to the cookhouse, especially for bully-beef stew, but the local people were sympathetic and invited us for meals.

Eventually rumour became reality. I was sitting in a London Park when the Second World War was declared. Now my job was to supervise the incoming Reservists and provide them with accommodation.

They came in their hundreds and bedded-down wherever there was a foot of space, even in the latrines. For many it was straight under canvas on Salisbury Plain where home comforts consisted of a lot of beer and bawdy songs. Studies for my Army First were abandoned as were many other things; even discipline temporarily went by the board.

Kitted up with pack mess-tins, water bottles, .303 rifles from the First World War and live ammunition, they were ready for action and marched forming fours in civvies (some in bowler hats) to the train terminal for embarkation to Dieppe.

By the end of 1939 we returned to armoured vehicles, moving the tanks around noisily from one area to another to create a false impression for enemy reconnaissance, that we possessed more armour than we actually had.

One of a mixed squadron from many Regiments I was billeted in Lonsborough Hall, a spacious mansion close to Market Weighton commandeered for Military Exercises. When on flying-picket duty looking for German parachutists on the Wolds, I was sometimes struck rigid by midnight appearances of inquisitive wildlife. Off-duty time was spent mucking out the animals on a farm near to the village where the farmer's wife made beautiful hot cakes of dinner plate size with thick rashers of home-cured bacon in them. The village ladies opened a tea stall and, charging a penny a cup, made so much profit that the cakes came free.

We danced and sang until three in the morning in the church parish hall with no intoxicating liquor as there was no pub in the village. But this did not prevent Chalky White from spending the night in the latrines having fallen from the pole into six feet of 'umbala' and unable to obtain assistance owing to his high aroma.

Our final move was to Lamport in Nottinghamshire (also in the rain) where our billet was in a field of waist-high grass with no fresh water. Advised of our impending arrival the villagers had padlocked the water pumps. Much aggravation later and soaked to the skin we moved into some stables, averaging twelve men to a bucket of water for washing.

Although informed we would be embarking for a 'Top Secret' destination it was no secret to us: when marched through the village to receive our 'new issue' we returned wearing pith-helmets, carrying tropical kit. The field was a swamp when Winston Churchill reviewed us with the words 'You are going to fight an easy enemy.'

With tearful goodbyes to friendly locals we set sail from Liverpool in an ocean-going liner, SS *Duchess of Bedford*, for the Middle East.

2

THE SS *DUCHESS OF BEDFORD*

PULLING OUT of Liverpool Bay, the masts of several ships could be seen above the water-line. With U-Boat opposition and kippers for our first breakfast on board I felt somewhat bilious.

Proceeding down the Irish Sea escorted by HMS *Hermes* with two circling destroyers forming letter 'S' movements around us, we would eventually reach the Bay of Biscay intact. As the *Duchess* lived up to her 'rolling' reputation, we sat at a long table with bacon and eggs before us and the whole lot slid from starboard to port-side.

With stomachs upside down we also rolled as we rushed to our several boat-stations in answer to the 'action stations' call through the intercom. I was on the sun-deck with a good range of vision as aircraft roared overhead, but we heard no explosion to account for the smoke pouring from amidship about three decks below our mess-hall.

Formed up for boat drill, code messages flashed between the aircraft-carrier and destroyer-escort, but no urgent call came from the Unit Commanders, neither was any urgency visible among the crew. Suddenly we were covered with the contents of a flour bomb; the plane responsible bore the red, white and blue insignia. This action was pronounced a 'very useful exercise'.

As camouflage on the ship was non-existent, much of the clean white paint was blackened and we had the mess to clean up. The Commanding Officer, Sir William P— now ordered we be given 'Army tack' as a toughening-up process for action in the Western Desert. Army cooks moved into the lavish kitchens and it was stew, stew and more stew. As we became used to the ever-sloping decks of the liner, sea-sickness became a thing of the past, and sailing towards the equator we heard risqué stories of the liner's former days from the stewards.

While we were anchored for a time at Freetown, Sierra Leone, natives came alongside in canoes offering fruit, carvings and girls for the 'Tommies'. A few shinned up onto the forecastle but were immediately ejected by the deck police. They showed much enthusiasm diving for pennies in the inky water.

I gave a concert in the main first-class lounge, singing the popular songs of the day which incurred favourable looks from a female auxiliary nurse. I loved to sing and, invited by the Bandmaster, had previously entertained officers and their wives once my cavalry training was complete. This arrangement lasted two weeks and resulted in an offer to audition for the BBC which could not be accepted, but when available I had continued to sing solo with the band of the King's Own Hussars at the Garrison Theatre.

Leaving Sierra Leone all was quiet until we reached the Equator where Father Neptune took over the ship and everyone was ducked in the traditional though none too gentle manner. The first prize of five hundred unsmokeable cigarettes won in a deck game went over the side.

In the midst of all this we had the 'alarm for action stations' again but this time our escort HMS *Ajax* was in trouble. A U-Boat had been trailing us since leaving Gibraltar. Surfacing, he let fly with his cannon at *Ajax* who suffered damage to her bridge, but the gallant veteran evaded him and circled to bring herself between the submarine and the *Duchess*. *Ajax* let the submarine have all she had and soon it disappeared beneath the surface. The swell of waves around us was a sea of oil. The submarine could not have been more than five hundred yards away when she sank but *Ajax* continued to weave and drop depth charges just to be sure. The Captain then ordered full steam ahead for Cape Town. We continued eating burnt porridge and Irish stew, and playing deck quoits with 'Cape to Cairo' dung cigarettes as the eternal prizes. I dreamt of our final destination. Would we find any Turkish delight in the Western Desert or only the scarab, the dung beetle held sacred by ancient Egyptians?

Called before the CO I was told of my transfer on or soon after arrival at our destination. I was not happy to leave but was told to 'Smile, idiot, this is a transfer to the Intelligence Corps and your pay will increase even if you do not have to do the job.'

The rest of our voyage was without incident and in a very calm sea we successfully rounded the Cape of Good Hope into harbour in front of Table Mountain with a beautiful azure skyline behind it. Following a trail of destruction left by the Aussies the previous week, there was no reception for us when we disembarked.

Forming fours, we endeavoured to walk without rolling through the main street of Cape Town where girls cheered from office windows. At that time attention locally was focused on the rape of a bus-load of WAAFs by blacks on Table Mountain. Having visited the local cathedral built in pure white stone, our return to ship was through squalid native quarters built of mud and straw with little or no sanitation and the inhabitants were distinctly unfriendly. Detailed for Dock Police duties meant remaining vigilant for the rest of our stay to ensure no-one shinned down the mooring ropes. With the Afrikaners hostile to the lads in khaki we left Cape Town with no regrets.

We sailed into the Indian Ocean where the sunset of golden-red and orange deepening into indigo formed a colourful panorama. With vast shoals of flying fish glinting silver in the dying light of the sun it was romantic to lounge on the rail with the Scots brogue of the little auxiliary nurse for comfort.

We reached Mozambique Channel and Madagascar without trouble and it was good to see Comoro and Aldabra which were such a contrast from our next port of call looking, as it was called, 'Black Aden'. Not allowed to disembark, by this time we were grease spots with insufficient clean changes. In the Red Sea area salt tablets made us perspire more profusely with the temperature 120°F in the shade but there was no shade. 'All hands on deck' to acclimatize us to the sun and we were relieved on reaching Port Taufic to be told that after the Suez Canal we would be home and dry.

Our trip up the Canal was uneventful, just sand. Very narrow, it widened in places like inland lakes with a little greenery and intermittent palm trees. Beasts provided the motive power for wheels and water holes, and it seemed we were like that ourselves, running around in ever repeating circles with no objective in view. With constant cadre classes and weapon training on board our voyage had not been a pleasure cruise.

We landed at Port Said intact except for a half-dozen deserters at Cape Town and were loaded onto the train for Cairo with its own special smells and flies. Arab boys ran alongside shouting, 'eggs, bread', anxious to earn some 'ackers'. They were much more enterprising than we Westerners (until we learned the hard way in the desert). They hung onto the outside of the train causing long delays. The little nursing auxiliaries bade tearful farewells as they prepared to be transported by road to the hospital in the suburbs of Heliopolis, Cairo.

Our journey took us to Tel-el-Kebir, which had a well-kept

war cemetery, white crosses as far as the eye could see in all directions. A very slow trek took us to Abbassia Barracks in Cairo where we were eaten to death with bed bugs and caught sand-fly fever and gyppo tummy. There was a lot of 'char' and more cadre classes with orders called at tops of voices at diminutive figures in the distance. It was difficult to distinguish the orders being given with others bawling on either flank.

There was lots of weapon practice including the new Bren-gun from Czechoslovakia and first aid classes mostly on snake bites, my speciality. The intensity of the activity revealed our lack of experience at that time.

Of course we had the usual practical joker. Drill shorts with wide turn-ups that could be let down at night for protection against mosquitoes were issued. In a queue a lighted cigarette in mine resulted in dire effects on my person. Strangely, I did not appreciate the humour or the diversion caused.

I made friends with the natives including the *dhobie* boy who could not understand kindness. Mohammed was a small, likeable chap, who eventually told me he was the only support for his widowed mother. Befriending him and feeding him cakes from the NAAFI, I always received in return more laundry than I sent. I did good business also with the *char wallah*, and the fruit and tomato sellers who always had a bowl of Condey's fluid and water handy, to wash the fruit before handing it over.

Entertainment was an open-air cinema, where bugs lived in the basket chairs and ensured uncomfortable viewing. Camp concerts were very good and I remember a lusty baritone singing the popular undertaker song of the time, 'I'll walk beside you'.

Visiting Shepheards Hotel and the Polo Club I befriended a Swiss German – Herr Zinnicker – who worked for King Farouk as a head chemist. As we ordered afternoon tea he strongly advised I did not partake of the lush plates of strawberries and cream – a dysentery risk. He took me to meet his petite French-speaking wife, who gave me a standing invitation to their luxury flat at Kasr-el-Nil, close to the Egyptian Barracks of the same name.

They introduced me to their Sudanese servant, a very tall man in a fez dressed entirely in white, who insisted I should understand that he was Sudanese and not Egyptian. 'You have made a friend for life,' Herr Zinnicker told me. On a later visit to Cairo in early 1942, prior to leaving for the Far East, Herr Zinnicker gave me a treasured poem which I managed to keep concealed despite the most rigorous of Japanese searches, and which I carried throughout my service life:

> As thou goest, step by step,
> I will open up the way before thee –
> Child of my love, fear not the unknown morrow,
> Dread not the new demand life makes of thee;
> Thy ignorance doth hold no cause for sorrow
> Since what thou knowest not is known to me.
> Thou canst not see today the hidden meaning
> Of my command, but thou the light shall gain.
> Walk on in faith, upon my promise leaning,
> And as thou goest, all shall be made plain.
> One step thou seest – then go forward boldly,
> One step is far enough for faith to see;
> Take that, and thy next duty shall be told thee,
> For step by step the Lord is leading thee.
> Stand not in fear thy adversaries counting,
> Dare every peril save to disobey.
> Thou shall march on, all obstacles surmounting
> For I, the Strong will open up the way.
> Wherefore go gladly to the task assigned thee.

Having my promise, needing nothing more
Than just to know, where'er the future find thee,
In all thy journeying I go before.

In the meantime little Alex, one of our gunner operators, had paid a visit to the Pyramids and returned with bites as big as golf balls on his face, hands and arms. It was obvious he had gone underground and we never did find out what bit him, but at last we left Abbassia Cairo and the flies for Mersa Matruh first stop, and then Bardia.

3

ACTION IN THE WESTERN DESERT

PROUDLY wearing the Desert Rat flashes on our sleeves, the Regulars were now ready for battle, our first encounter with the Italian enemy. For two days in blistering heat we followed the coast road in convoy, then stopped to organize, fill machine-gun belts and ensure no supplies or vehicles had been lost, especially with overheating.

We were fanned-out at last, with no more slit-trench digging for a while nor, hopefully, scorpions. Attending to a private matter I was caught out in the open by Italian planes who managed to hit three Bedfords complete with crews. We had to keep moving, and the flies had already rediscovered us when we met the scarabs. They swarmed, rolling little golf balls of our excreta up the sand dunes.

Trading tea for eggs we never saw a chicken but confused the Arabs and got more than our fair share while they made off happily with a half mug of dry tea. As fresh water was not available, urine in the radiators had to do for boiling eggs.

One Arab encounter involved us in a war with the Bedouins, who we forced into untying their horses and ponies which were too tightly hobbled. I acquired my own pet at this time, a lizard called Sammy who accompanied me on night patrols sitting around my shoulder.

Then Ramadan came, lasting forty days and nights. My job was to make sure the Bedouin cooking-fires, which they lit in a triangle around our bivouac at night, were extinguished to prevent us from becoming sitting targets. Invited into their huge tents I was offered bread and refreshment out of salmon tins which they prized like ancestral silver. Breaking bread or chipatties one becomes a blood-brother and has access to the Chief's possessions, including wives, but a plea of tiredness was necessary so as not to offend.

For several reasons we had to break with the coast road and among the rocky terrain of the Western Desert following the escarpment I saw my first mirage, purple with buildings and palm trees. We stopped the convoy to deploy the vehicles for the long night (there is no twilight in Egypt). Pinky spread the tarpaulin to cover us for the night to prevent us being soaked, as a small lake of dew had formed between each sleeper in the mornings. Before retiring Pinky uselessly tried to dig a slit trench but about an inch below the surface it was solid. With no primus stove, we cut down a four-gallon drum, half filled it with sand and soaked the sand with petrol.

Supply vehicles reached the convoy intermittently, but our water cart with distilled sea water had been shot up. This was a regular occurrence throughout the campaign. The odd tin of sausages did get through but in the absence of cash were booked to be deducted from pay. With petrol dumps all over the place the RASC had done a good job but had forgotten that men also require fuel.

Apart from the eggs there were creatures in the desert but not a lot were palatable. One could suck the camel thorn which grew profusely while showing no sign of life at all. There were of course the pyards, syphilitic piebald dogs, howling love calls all night long. Wild camels exuded rotten fish smells and to cap all of this, our clothes had to be washed in petrol. By now we were a dirty, scruffy, unshaven lot. Pinky examined blistered hands in disgust and the dirt did nothing for his complexion; my own was like rawhide and just got blacker under the desert camouflage, for the sand was like powdered cement. Tapping the third valve of the tank radio gave us the BBC (broken biscuit corporation) so we were able to keep up with the news and knew how old it was by our reported movements. It was around this time that fellow singer Al Bowley was killed in a bombing raid on London. He had been a favourite of Forces and girls alike. Nostalgia made sentimental cusses of us all.

One of our group was Dolly Pratt, a wild, bloodshot-eyed, black-haired man with dirty rolled-up shorts, rolled-down socks and a heavy tan. He was a good mechanic and likeable apart from his lethal necklace. Around his neck he had a length of fuse wire and about every inch hung a scorpion like 'A String of Pearls'.

An air raid by Italian Fiats sent us rushing for the crater left by the bomb, me pushing Dolly in with a rugby tackle. I was struck by a massive piece of rock and Dolly emerged grinning with scorpions still intact around his neck. The planes were so low that one of our gunners sitting in his tank cleaning the machine-gun was amazed to see a Fiat in the sights. As the gun was built-in on the turret it had little elevation, but he pulled the trigger and put paid to the enemy.

Just as the raid started a bunch of Free French Infantry stragglers had arrived to ask for our assistance. Amid sulphur fumes and flying rocks, great banks of sand rose twenty to thirty feet in the air. We stayed in that position two more days. Dolly carved a lovely cross for the dead Free French who had died in the raid, all the more remarkable as he was not a bit religious. It was the first blood spilt in our presence.

As a reconnaissance unit we were given a free hand to discover enemy position, strategic features and manpower strength. As the Italians were excellent in the art of camouflage, to have used our two Lysander aircraft would not have been profitable. With some knowledge of minelaying it was decided to strike for the south rather than north to our prime objective of Mersa Matruh. At this point Sammy bit the hand that fed him so I let him go.

The sand was much softer as we proceeded south towards Libya and, always in danger of bogging down, we asked for volunteers to walk ahead: not a favourite occupation among our dysentery-ridden group. The weekly visit by the 'Doc' was the sole medical attention and large doses of castor oil were unceremoniously administered without any choice. Wilby was the volunteer until he kicked what appeared to be an old tin can (one of many murderous gadgets used by the Italians); the anti-personnel mine did its job and got Wilby on his way home minus half a foot.

Moving mostly at night, navigating by the stars over rough tracks (whose we did not know), we often caught the smell of death and the even stronger odour of wild camel.

Stopping to camouflage the vehicles and being desperate for food we had a bright idea and took the Bedford eight-hundred-weight hunting, finding a gazelle. Egypt however did not support such lovely creatures; we had strayed further than we thought into Libya. It was here that we encountered very colourful Arabs dressed in blues and greens with red sashes, swords and daggers, who escorted us to an oasis (straight out of *Desert Song*).

Right here in the middle of nowhere sat a corrugated tin hut. In about ninety degrees in the shade but hotter inside, a neatly dressed Salvation Army Captain served us with mugs of hot steaming tea. We never discovered who he or his customers were; he cheerfully made us welcome yet barely spoke a word as we gulped down the tea. Without further incident we found our way back to an anxious troop. The pyards circled us as they knew we had raw meat; we had another name for them: 'shite hawks'.

At last our Brigade air cover arrived, four clacked-out Gladiator biplanes, canvas and wood, silvery in the sunlight with no 'drome to go to. I had flown in one of these museum pieces in 1932 and they crashed, tired and old-aged, even then.

> England my Island home,
> Land of the free,
> England unconquered yet
> O'er land and sea,
> England my Island home,
> Answer my prayer,
> God keep Britannia's sons,
> Lords of the Air . . .

With the move on, wireless silence was imminent and as night fell we bivouacked hoping for rest but an almighty roar began to pass over us as the clamour of guns lit the sky. It was mainly a Naval barrage on our target of Mersa Matruh. The Italians responded with tracers but had nothing to match the Royal Navy. After what seemed like hours it was silent. This time the Australian Infantry were sent in first, with us now relegated from our usual reconnaissance, doing the mopping up at first light.

There was a constant fight for survival in the desert, no home comforts and not a decent uniform between us. When we reached Mersa I acquired a lovely brown civilian suit from an Italian journalist with the tab inside reading 'Made in Roma'. Some of the lads got into Italian Air Force uniforms, comfortable serge, so easy to wear after our unrecognizable dirty drill. We did not linger long in the extreme cold, but pushing on into the town we took more prisoners than we could feed.

Mussolini's Black Shirt Brigade were putting up strong pockets of resistance as were his crack Alpine Troops, picturesque in their greenish uniforms and cocked hats with feathered plumes, more like Swiss peasants in *The Sound of Music*.

With the whole place booby-trapped, rank carried little weight in such circumstances. The little private concerns himself with immediate responsibilities. In our case it was our small circle of vehicle crews, three men to each of three vehicles, and beyond that all was alien.

We now experienced a process of change towards our fellow-man, nothing to do with religion or high thoughts, but motivated by reliance upon each other for survival. We received no directive from higher authority in Cairo, not even a Padre was sent, only two Army Scripture readers who lay down beside us in the battle line, prayed and read the Bible aloud.

On the third day we rose. Our vehicle hit a mine and the driver had his legs blown off in the driving seat. It could have been anyone of us whose turn it was to drive.

Returned by the supply truck was a parcel of goodies sent by Rowntrees for one of their employees, which kept going the rounds because he was not with us. Finally we opened it and shared it between us. By now our larder consisted of only six or seven pounds of flour.

General Wavell drove up to the front in a beautiful silver Rover. Immaculate in starched drill, red-tabbed lapels and gold braid on his peaked cap he had no escort. I always remember the eye-patch he wore, it so resembled that of Moshe Dayan. Aware of our inferior equipment he said he felt like a mother hen forsaking his brood, but promised us fresh bread and vegetables.

This brought to mind one of the many songs my mother taught me as a child:

> It's only a little box of soldiers
> Only a few, that's all,
> When they're up, there ain't half enough,
> But they're all manufactured of the real good stuff.
> England's the name of the box they're in
> And when Britannia plays with her little box of soldiers
> She plays the game to win.

After reconnoitring Mersa Matruh we had plans to push on to Bardia. We found an abandoned motorcycle on the road to Sidi-Barrani and one of the troops, deciding to test it, lost his life as it was booby-trapped. Italian range-finders and spotters, perched up what appeared to be telegraph poles, became easy targets and were short lived.

General Wavell's strategy of going around the enemy's flank paid off, saving many lives, but the Australian Infantry (either from lack of experience or from enthusiasm) suffered great losses. They were better equipped if not as well disciplined. (They always had sand-coloured marquees and Anchor butter, but were not too fond of us 'Limeys'.)

On Christmas Day 1940 we tuned into the BBC where the announcer was telling folks back home not to worry about the Eighth Army as they were all enjoying Christmas. We had no letters from home, and with restrained tears we viewed our food stock which I decided to make into a pudding on our invented primus stove. Ingredients: six pounds of flour with weevils, and rancid distilled water. A message from GHQ read that parcels would be a little late. I received mine in February 1941, a shoebox full of popcorn and a nine-foot long khaki scarf, which

I swapped for a balaclava, it being more adequate for the freezing conditions.

After our riotous Christmas we moved on for Salum and thence to Bardia on the Libyan plateau, and amid shot and shell took more prisoners than we could cater for. Many had frost-bite, but with no medical equipment or food, we could only encircle them and put vehicle festoon lights on at night to fool them into thinking we were awake. With the big push on, prisoners had to be left without food or assistance. The promised bread and vegetables arrived, the bread had sand right through the middle but this did not deter us, although the cabbage had seen better days; it was yellow and rotted.

Leaving Mersa I found an Australian infantryman in an almost burnt-out hut, but could only cover his third-degree burns with violet acriflavine before having to leave him.

At El Bomba the Arabs were lined up but not for concealing arms. The supply of machine-gun belts prepared by the Egyptian Army had been sabotaged.

Finally the HIT descended into our midst with sudden devastation. The intensity meant we had to abandon vehicles, and sprawl in the sand watching the massive shell explosions. There were the heavies, and seeing all vehicles on fire and hearing screams, troops ran in all directions trying to smother flames from clothing. With total confusion reigning I ran from exploding ammunition and slid into a shell hole. Crawling again for an eternity I found refuge in what I later discovered to be a very small two-man enemy tank, and climbing into the turret fell into a deep stupor, awakening to find myself a prisoner of the Italian front-line Infantry who had been involved with the fighting bombardment of the Squadron.

The dust had lifted and the guards did not speak but the Corporal-Major was friendly. He was a grubby little man in untidy blue uniform who would take us to his depot at Fort Mkhili when transport could be found, a major problem that concerned him for his own men. His destination was a hundred mile trek away, not practical in that terrain with frugal water supplies. I said I had a bearing, but his orders were to take all prisoners to the Black Shirt Garrison at Mkhili. Commonsense prevailed and we set off for the Italian Air Force base about twenty kilometres away. I suspected we would find the Australians there. The burnt-out smoking vehicles around us – both British and Italian – was evidence of heavy losses on both sides. When I asked for news of my troop, the little Major told me, 'All Tommies die.'

This was the beginning of the battle for Tobruk. After many halts the sun made it impossible to continue. The Major held discussions with his Company about capitulation. He handed his rifle and bayonet to me saying 'Signor, we your prisoners,' and ceremoniously his men laid down their arms. We took a rifle each and plenty of ammunition, burying the rest, and forming columns of four went forward.

There were roughly ten miles left to El Adem. In due course we crept cautiously up to the nearest ridge and peeped over. To our delight we saw three large orange marquees and some well-dressed men in desert uniforms with sloppy bush hats. Stumbling over the ridge-threshold I showed my identity tags to the Sergeant who whistled us over to one of the tents where we found all the refreshments we needed. It was like discovering gold at Klondyke and we wasted no time in eating all we were offered, momentarily forgetting our eleven prisoners.

Asking to see the Colonel, I was granted permission after a long interval. Without hesitation he said, 'Shoot the bastards.' Not pleading, I said, 'But they are all excellent cooks, Sir.' After careful thought, he agreed to take them. The last I saw of them, they were getting stuck into the field kitchen after profuse thanks and we parted good friends.

The Australians told us Tobruk had fallen and we could have transport to El Adem. As we descended into the bunkers under El Adem airfield a familiar voice upbraided me with, 'Where the hell have you been?' It was our Squadron Leader De Wend. 'You have missed the fun and hard work and the typist is dead. I want some Part II Orders out right now.' A portable typewriter full of sand was thrown into my lap. When he eventually received the Military Cross he lined us all up and said, 'It belongs to you, gentlemen.'

A man who earned but never received recognition was Major Bonham-Carter, a remarkable navigator. He stood up in his little unprotected jeep, swaying from lack of sleep, scurrying endlessly along as he guided his squadron through shot, shell and mine-fields on our route in January 1941, his Herculean figure standing out against the landscape. I salute him as an unsung hero of the Western Desert.

Tobruk was a shambles. In one air raid shelter deep in the bowels of the earth I found stinking corpses. The Medical Corps were too far back to assist. Housed in marquees about thirty miles from the main base the wounded travelled over hundreds of miles in field ambulances for treatment. I thought of my little red rose: 'The Red Cross Nurse.'

> There's the one red rose
> A soldier knows,
> And it's wonderful to see,
> Though it's wet with tears
> It will live for years
> In my garden of memory.
> It's the one red rose

24

The soldier knows,
It's the work of a master's hand.
In the war's great curse
Stood the red cross nurse
The rose of No Man's Land.

Our reconnaissance Squadron re-formed and we made our way to Fort Mkhili, traversing the Derna Pass with buzzards circling in anticipation. This would be our first encounter with the Black Shirts who would meet us head on with superior M13 tanks. Opposition at the Pass was slight. It had been blown in the middle of the S-shaped climb of the Heights, but our Royal Engineers had been hard at work to meet our deadline. They bridged the back and opened the way to Mkhili.

Then we were blasted to hell by our own Royal Air Force. Licking our wounds, and burying the dead, we were convinced the RAF were fifth column quislings for betraying our positions, and nicknamed them Riff-Raff. Now my lovely brown suit from Roma was bloody and ruined. Two weeks later the RAF dropped a typed message apologising for their devastating raid. I suppose we must forgive them, for we would all look like Riffs from the air. Whatever the difficulties we must go forward. The supply vehicles came up to the Front once a week to pay us an honorary visit, when the pettiness of our beloved QM was decidedly irksome. A bully-boy, he was chicken underneath and would not get out of his slit-trench at the request of the Squadron Leader.

— 4 —

FURTHER ACTION

A DESPATCH came over the air with instructions to me to report to Fort Mkhili. I guessed that my next assignment was to be a glorified messenger boy (later confirmed in the jungles of Java). Clothed in smelly Bedouin smock and head-dress I had to lose myself; no transport, no map, no dogtags and Arabic too classical to pass muster. My goodbyes said at night, I had only the Lord for guidance.

Luckily I fell in with a camel train bound for Mkhili although it struck me that it was going in the wrong direction. They should have been moving away from the impending battle zone. Abdiani (Abdul) became my guide and brother. He was tall, strong and colourfully dressed (as were most Libyans). My friendship could have been short-lived as I foolishly offered piastres which were promptly dropped and spat upon. This was a time when I could have wept. Travelling with the Feudal Bedouins I had to become an Arab. A silent Abdul fed and watered me, protected me from those less charitable to strangers in their midst and as I had no camel often carried me too.

During the course of our journey we came upon the sight of tanks 'in lines of battle' but unmanned. They were not tanks at all but inflatable dirigibles very effective in deceiving the enemy, especially from the air. Advising Abdul to tell the train: 'Ignore it and press on', we cautiously approached a planter's bungalow

26

in the 'cultivated zone' but it was deserted. It was night; groping around the main room for booby traps I found none and slept till the following midday. The Bedouins remained outside – fortunately for them for on awakening I found my bedroom floor was covered in excrement.

In Cyrenaica proper I conveyed to Abdul my anxiety that the fifty-mile trek from Derna to Mkhili was taking too long (although I was not in any great hurry to arrive). He indicated with a stick in the sand that we were about ten miles away and it would be safer to arrive by moonlight. I agreed. Our arrival had to be postponed for twenty-four hours as the warships off the coast began a horrific bombardment over our heads towards our destination, Mkhili. I hoped my 'contact' at the Fort had survived the onslaught.

The night was well lit by the moon as we approached Fort Mkhili. Tired and bedraggled, our gaze became riveted, almost directly into the gun-barrels of Black Shirt Artillery standing motionless in their positions as far as the eye could see. It was a macabre scene as we cautiously approached the rows of static figures. Then realization dawned that they were dead. The Bedouins pounced. They robbed and mutilated the immaculate bodies of our enemy to a sickening degree and brought to mind the vulnerability of our own Field Artillery.

With the carnage over, insignificant amounts of goods were loaded onto the camels. Ignoring the arms and ammunition every Bedouin had a watch, including Abdul, and his watch featured the tides, moon and stars.

My orders were to re-establish contact with a Don Giovanni but not a soul could be found in the shambles that was Mkhili, I hoped he had escaped. Having had my fill of trotting around the desert I left for Benghazi to join whatever unit was there. How civilized to find the Command and Units housed in Italian

27

concrete bunkers as if they had been there for months. The streets were deserted of civilians who hid behind shuttered windows; only the Police were in evidence. The great blue mosaic archway with a gold eagle centrepiece led to the docks but its beauty was marred by the carnage below. Women had been thrown to the ground from top windows by Australians unable to have their way.

Regrouping for El Agheila we were given M13 Italian tanks and instructed to bury them up to the turrets and use them as gun emplacements if they broke down. The best equipment was deployed to Greece. Waiting-man to go to Crete I was disgusted to hear some officers debating whether to take cricket bats. I could still remember the waxworks of Mkhili.

We travelled by road to El Agheila passing burnt-out vehicles and small black crosses. Someone had taken the time to bury their dead and fashion crosses out of transport debris, but my heart sank because the havoc wreaked by the Stuka dive-bombers was upon Bedford 3-tonners. Because we were using 'enemy' vehicles German reconnaissance patrols ignored us.

As Rommel's forces would soon be on the attack we dug in the M13s to wait while Rommel played cat and mouse. We had no supplies and could only watch the shite hawks and the enemy planes patrolling between El Agheila and Benghazi. We built bivouacs in the sand from burnt-out vehicles and indeed felt like the Army of forgotten men; we did not even have the tools to fight an effective war. The rumblings of the German Panzers became louder but the useless M13s were now abandoned and we went forward on foot.

All this time poor old Abdul had hung on like a pet dog and would not leave me, but he now disappeared to seek his own clansmen. Other 'Arabs' had entered our bivouacs but with fair beards; I believe they were Germans in disguise.

With soft Cyrenaican sand in our shoes we plodded to Tripolitania as if born to the desert. Tunisia would be our next stop so we about-faced and lived on what we could find. We came upon a Bedford truck (not service) loaded with pineapple chunks which we ate until we were indeed square. In miles of nothingness and not a living soul, all we saw were more black crosses. Our next find was an Italian desert vehicle on huge high wheels. It was operative and loaded with Nestle's milk, with a little pink bird on the labels.

We travelled by night and lay under the vehicle during the day as we did not know how close the Germans were. After repassing the little crosses we bypassed Benghazi as it was in flames, and headed for Derna, which was occupied by Reich forces. As we were in an Italian vehicle they still did not challenge us.

The journey through the steep winding pass was dangerous in the moonlight but, dodging in and out of the 'cultivated zone' to evade the Panzers, we got through. Being an infiltrator without a radio or supplies was not a comfortable situation to be in. With no compass we reached Tobruk by chance, but could not get through the perimeter. My comrade prayed beside me and had his head blown off; he was not a religious man so must have had a premonition. I carried his remains to the wire which was parted by some Aussie squaddies and I walked with my load to some caves that seemed to be inhabited.

Amazingly, I was confronted by my Squadron Leader De Wend, squatting on a rock, clean and shining with gleaming Sam Browne. Everyone else was scruffy and apparently undisciplined, brewing up coal-black tea in filthy dixies and frying beans on improvised stoves. The smell almost killed me; I had not seen a soya bean in months.

The alarm sounded for action-stations and I was quickly

ushered outside again. Within the ranks there was an immediate transformation, as within seconds the Stukas arrived with a vengeance. The reason for being outside was apparent when the roof of the cave bounced under the strain of the bombing: exposure to the Stukas was preferable to being buried alive. Everyone rushed to their posts ready to have a go in British Bulldog tradition. A captured anti-aircraft gun at the top of the caves was wielded by the Squadron cook with fervour. A diving Stuka dropped whistling bombs. It was piloted by a young boy: I saw his face, fair haired, he was smirking. All around, men were losing life and limbs in the unabating raid. As the last of our four Spitfires was shot down I took my usual route in emergencies. A jolt hit my lumber region in clouds of sand as I jumped into a crater.

Unable to take Tobruk, Rommel had cut off the movement of supplies except those by sea, from which constantly moving landing barges could be used. In the harbour the Italian cruiser *Gratzianni* lay on its side. In the quiet that followed, my demise was announced but crawling along I dragged myself back to the caves thinking, 'Heaven can't be like this.'

The following morning Squadron Leader De Wend lined us all up (we looked rather like Chinese coolies) and, indicating his own gleaming Sam Browne, said: 'This is what I want you to get back to.'

The Aussies had gone on strike until Winston sent them a cargo of Anchor beer so now it was up to the 'Limeys'. With the German Haubitze Howitzers installed on railway lines across the harbour we were held in an iron grip by land, sea and air. A good number of troops were evacuated, crammed onto barges and protected by one lonely frigate. That day the Mediterranean looked like the North Sea, brown and cold, with huge waves pounding the sides of the ship. There was a submarine warning but no-one had lifejackets as we proceeded past the sunken cruiser without a backward glance. After our departure the South Africans took over Tobruk and lost it to the Afrika Korps commanded by Rommel.

Sailing a zig-zag course we arrived safely in Alexandria and thence by train to Cairo, with Arabs as usual hanging onto the sides and roof of the train. Looking forward to a 'refit', bloodstained and horrible to look at, I slept all the way to Cairo.

At Abbassia Barracks, with five days leave and anxious to see my contacts Professor Fakhoury and the Zinnickers, I was struck down with double pneumonia. Somehow making my way to Heliopolis I was cared for by my friends. The Professor used a methylated spirit-lamp to heat meat paste jars, and applied them to my chest and back to draw off fluid. It undoubtedly saved my life for I was much improved in two days.

News came through that our escort HMS *York* had been torpedoed off Crete on 2 May 1941.

Cairo was a hot-bed of intrigue and illegal activities. It was certainly anti-British. Prostitution was rife, with instructions 'not to taste the toffee without the wrapper' largely ignored. Drugs were a valuable currency for obtaining information though I had no stomach for nefarious subversion.

Dressed as an Arab to avoid suspicion, I was taken by the Professor to the Faculty of Science to witness happenings that could not have occurred without the knowledge of the Egyptian Government. A tunnelling operation was taking place to undermine the Abbassia Garrison which would have blown up about ten thousand troops. If successful it would have enabled Rommel to proceed to the Suez unhindered.

I returned to Heliopolis with Professor Fakoury, who contacted Army Intelligence, and for two successive days I was interrogated at his residence about the activity I had witnessed.

A 15 cwt unmarked truck awaited in the grounds of a Military Hospital to which I was transferred, and I left Cairo with a low-flying Hurricane circling over it all the way to Port Suez for my protection.

PART TWO

5

MISSION IN PALEMBANG AND THE

HEADHUNTERS

THE SHIP I boarded at Port Suez flew the Norwegian flag, had very uncomfortable hammocks, lousy food and no relaxation activities. A respite for me during that boring journey was to give lectures on snake bites. On reaching Ceylon the Squadron Leader gave us the choice of going to Australia or, for the honour and glory of the Regiment, to go to the Dutch East Indies.

Choosing honour and glory, by a small majority, we were dropped into Palembang by Lancaster with instructions to destroy the oil refinery. My free-fall experience proved helpful. We advanced with some success but, having no supplies, were reduced to grovelling for peanuts (like mushy peas). With mosquitoes in abundance the chaps began to sicken with malaria. It was an escapade to the six of us but conditions were against us with everything on the attack, including red ants. Wild pineapples shredded our clothing, and Stew Wilson's unsuccessful climb for coconuts scraped his flesh to the bone.

It was no picnic and although the refinery did not expect a raid they put up resistance with four-fives and light weaponry. Our orders were explicit: 'Kill them so none could aid the Japanese.' There were no children but unhappily there were a few native women. Heavy-hearted from the spilling of innocent blood we buried our only casualty, making a cross and saying a prayer. Leaving behind a blazing mass of twisted metal and carrying as much food as we could (most of it was lost in the swamp), we hacked our way through to Ousthaven, a little port in Sumatra. Some of the men developed ringworm. Tropical parasites penetrated beneath the skin and the temperature over 100°F grew more humid. Seeing an aged baboon sitting on the branch of a tree crying its heart out, I was deeply moved.

Aware that we were being watched but too tired to care, we observed a motley lot of Sumatran natives hidden behind the foliage. We approached what appeared to be the leader who stepped forward with a huge grin, threw down a scimitar in front of me, then knelt down. We took this for friendship, unaware that the natives had witnessed our activities at the refinery. They had circled us in the jungle, then waited for us. Had they chosen to turn on us we would not have survived.

In an alien place with no jungle lore and beset by mosquitoes and leeches I was sick with delirium. I did not know if I crawled, walked or was carried to Djambi – one hundred miles in the wrong direction. I sweated in a native hut tended by a woman, maybe for the pot, but, vomiting at both ends, only needed the kazi.

They carried me outside on a litter but I struggled to my swollen 'Singapore' feet in alarm. I was led to the head-man who grinned and slowly drew his weapon shouting 'Nippon!' Facing me, he raised his scimitar with a blood curdling yell, bringing it crashing down onto a log close to my feet, cutting it clean in half. His whole retinue sharpened weapons and simulated a mock battle.

My companions were being bathed by local maidens and my turn soon followed. These natives were small and non-hostile. In a sign language they taught us how to make straw sandals and to bind our sores with banana leaves. They were ready to share even their wives but we had no appetite. My need was for word of home and I wondered why none had ever reached me.

It became apparent that the natives were preparing for a long trek. They planned to meet 'Nippon' head on at their landing, likening them in their ignorance to a rival tribe out looting. Playfully brandishing scimitars in front of us they intimated that five of us, covered in rashes and filled with dysentery, should accompany them. Leaving behind old men, women and children to keep guard we also left Wally with 'Java Balls' (medics note: testicles swollen out of proportion).

Using an in-built compass I judged we were moving due east which would be a fifty mile trek to the coast. I had the mad thought that we could get a boat and reach Singapore about one hundred and fifty miles north-east. We still had arms strong enough to paddle but it was a pipe dream, as events revealed. Our companions battled against the jungle, slashing and flailing at the undergrowth with their sharpened blades. I thought of the Regimental motto of 'Nec Aspera Terrente' – 'Let Nothing Deter' and wished myself at Tidworth turning over 'that tank'.

We encountered huge mammals and crocodiles and a large anthropoid ape who raged in fury at our invasion was distressingly cut down by the natives. They had no aversion to killing, obviously because of the need to survive in the tropical jungle. We ate 'mack-mack' birds (an obscene forbidden word in Malaya), which were not birds but tree lizards with skins like a rhinoceros but with tasty entrails. Expertly guided from the swamps, I now counted the hours.

In two days we reached the ocean and made camp to await the enemy. The beach was desolate: no wood, ship or boat. Vastly outnumbered we waited while under close observation.

At dusk three or four small boats appeared, hand-propelled by

1. The Headhunters.

oars. Assuming these to be the enemy they were set upon by the natives as they reached the shore, the blood-letting only taking minutes. Limping to the water's edge I was filled with horror; they were not Japanese but white men, women and children, about fifty altogether, one saying 'Singapore' as he died. Unashamedly I wept; they had endured much to escape the Japanese only to end this way. All these years later I am still sick at heart by its recollection.

Robbing the corpses, the natives danced around setting fire to our means of escape, the precious boats with names like *Beau Geste* and *Liverpool* on their hulls. The conquerors then intimated their intention to return to Djambi as we turned our backs on that horrific scene. We made it quite clear we would not go back. We must get to Ousthaven at all speed and arrange for our companion to be picked up.

Squatting with our headhunting chief (this we had witnessed) he drew a map in the earth to indicate the port. Although primitive he did not lack intelligence and promptly called his warriors to Council. He pointed to me and made what I now know to be a gesture of friendship, then, waving his arm in a big circle, pointed south.

I realized they agreed to escort us to the rendezvous, two hundred miles from their own destination. Perhaps it was our unwholesome reek that formed their affinity towards us but we gratefully accepted their help. Having rested for a considerable time, it felt like a nightmare when with difficulty I rose, still delirious, with a one hundred mile trek ahead, and glimpsed eternity. Determined to find civilization I mustered my inner resources. It was peace and love I wanted but I never did find my Shangri-La.

Retracing our way to Palembang, trekking through the jungle, sometimes carried, we would never have survived without the tireless efforts of our little friends. Gathering strength from who knows where, we pushed on, hopeful that we would not meet the Japanese, for by now we could imagine the fate of those in Singapore. The escapers were never far from my thoughts.

We reached Baturadja ready for a rest but dared not do so as the enemy were close behind us, so we pushed on to the port of Telukbetung. On arrival we were dismayed to see it had been shelled from the sea as we caught the tail-end of the bombardment. With sinking hearts we realized that the boats in harbour were either upside down or burning. Escape was impossible yet still our friends stayed to scavenge, so at least we would survive. Impervious to the shellfire they yelled and danced with each blasting shell. Oblivious to danger, they did not suffer even one fatality.

We turned due east, me trundling along behind Smudger, when with a flash and a terrific roar his right leg was severed to the knee. I tried to stem the flow of blood with a crude tourniquet using the remains of my germ-ridden shirt while the natives continued to yell terpsichorally. We remaining four were not fit to carry Smudger so he and I set off on a three-legged race. For a seeming age we rested to stem the bloodflow. In great pain, he was acutely aware of the gravity of our predicament. Weaponless, we could only hope to run into our own lads fighting rearguard actions.

With trepidation we moved on and fifteen miles from our goal met an RAF squadron, now 'Infantry Converts' to fight a rearguard action. They had landed at Ousthaven with enormous sea kit-bags to clear the jungle for an airstrip. This was a blatant sacrifice by the upper echelons in their pipe-dream of establishing a military presence in defence of the islands. Smartly dressed in fresh blue uniforms, the ground staff of the famous

Squadron Leader Douglas Bader welcomed us and did their best to feed and clothe us. Watching from the distance, our natives suddenly whooped and disappeared forever. Refusing to leave Smudger, we set off for the waterfront leaving the lads in blue to dig themselves in.

6

BATAVIA TO BANDUNG

AFTER endless days and nights living on wild pineapples, coconuts and mushy peanuts, under constant attack from curtains of mosquitoes, we were all turning green with malaria as we returned to Ousthaven, collecting dregs of humanity along the way.

The SS *Tigress* was such a welcome sight but with indiscriminate shooting around we all joined in to help evacuees get away. Chaos reigned and the elderly Dutch lady I was supporting was shot in the thigh. After all the confusion it was with relief we boarded the remaining coaster and slid out of port with no protection into the black night. Not even a machine gun, and six million Nips on our tail.

As my companion moaned, cries of anguish from the injured continued. Within a mile or so disaster struck when a loud explosion occurred followed by a roar and in minutes we were in a mêlée of oil and sea water.

I awoke at dawn floating on a piece of driftwood in a calm sea. I remembered trying to help a woman in the heaving polluted waters but she had disappeared. The destroyers in the Straits flew the Japanese flag. Oblivious to the need to rescue, they passed in line astern like a fleet of taxis.

An eternity later I was dragged by the hair from the sea and lashed to the rigging of what turned out to be a tiny coaster crammed with humanity. The food when it appeared perhaps two days later was from two steaming cauldrons stirred by unkempt native boys and proved to be inedible rice and tea leaves. There were over three hundred on board but not all had been rescued from the sea; some were Malay-coolies *en route* to Java plantations. Like gypsies they hibernated around the islands, weary of their roaming.

With no pilot guidance we pulled into a small cove rife with coral reefs and as the Captain was taking his cargo no further, despite disabilities we were invited to jump overboard. So far my schoolboy fantasies of the South Seas had not appeared.

The swim ashore was refreshing in the surf and we were greeted on the shore by a mob of Dutch, Javanese and, surprisingly, English. Meanwhile the ship had moored at a small jetty, much to our annoyance. It had been a joke on the Captain's part to make us swim although I suppose he had been under no obligation to rescue us.

Stumbling along the jetty, hoping to muscle in on some food, I met some 'Tommies' who were waiting for the Dutch Military to house and feed us. I knew of the British Tommies' ingenuity in hard times. We had strange table fellows in the Western Desert who squatted down and passed on with no questions asked, but such was not the case here.

Suddenly I was held in a very tight female grip and planted with a kiss. The Fräulein I rescued had recognized me. She had been rescued from the life-raft I put her on by a small patrol boat which then crept across the straits under cover of darkness. We were both glad to find each other alive. She told me she was the Civil Administrator for the whole of the Sumatra region. Some responsibility for a woman, especially in headhunter country!

Just worn out survivors and defenceless fishermen in the port, we were soon bombarded from the sea and air by a 'Navyo' with machine guns and bombs taking their death toll. Again I protected my Fräulein, smothering her beneath me from the flying shrapnel. With our numbers now halved food was not our prime thought. At least we survived but because of the confusion, alas, we never knew each other's name. Tall, slim and very beautiful she shivered from head to foot as we stepped across the dead and dying on the jetty. We had walked for about a mile when we were picked up by Dutch soldiers in jungle-greens and placed on ox carts to be taken to their railhead several miles away. Taking no notice of my Fräulein's gestures towards me they led her off to more elaborate transport and too far from me to be able to speak so I blew her a farewell kiss.

At the railhead, VIPs went in coaches, with the rest of us in open trucks. A solitary Jap Navyo strafed us, chased by a monstrous beer-barrel shape displaying the RAF red, white and blue. I learned later it was the Brewster Buffalo, but the superior Navyo, somersaulting, shot it in half. I ran along beside the coaches to see if my companion was hurt; she waved excitedly but we were not permitted to speak.

Eventually housed in Batavia, now Djakarta, in native huts with rush roofs, we slept on long sleeping platforms along each side of the hut with no privacy at all. Within a short time we were supplied with uniforms, orders were issued in pre-war style and my first aid lectures on snake bites began again. Once complete, my services were dispensed with and despite Dutch promises to pay us in guilders I was left to my own devices without a sou to my name.

I had no map but must find my way to Bandung to complete my mission and deliver important documents to the HQ of General Wavell. Obeying orders was an inherent duty. Going down into Batavia I refused the potent doctored coconut fluid offered freely by shady operators, and moved to a small café.

With a brief-case strapped to my wrist, I rested, reserving

energy, but was unable to avoid the intense tropical heat. A huge figure in a white ducksuit and braided cap came and sat beside me. Speaking quietly he introduced himself as a Superintendent-in-Chief of the Salvation Army in the Netherlands East Indies. He was bound for Bandung. Reflecting that he would be an asset with the locals I told him I was making for Divisional Headquarters there, and readily accepted his invitation to travel with him. He explained that as bridges had been blown in anticipation of the Jap invasion we would have to go by foot and donkey cart. He wondered if I was up to the jungle hazards. I did not elaborate but told him that I was.

Inadequately equipped, we set off at once on slow yak carts, a very rough ride. The journey could take weeks but at least it was by cart. I kept a low profile but with my new friend in charge we were well treated. We abandoned the cart for the jungle and as before the mosquitoes and ants nipped while the leeches clung. I had been here before.

My companion's suit never got dirty, nor did he seem inclined to eat, but speculation was interrupted by the news that a tiger was on the prowl and had carried off a woman from one of the plantations. She had left her basket, which they never do. As tigers always follow the same tracks we bivouacked to await our quarry. Unarmed, the delay was frustrating, and it was debatable whether our greatest danger was from the tiger or the natives.

After several days we were awoken by the guards alerted by the roar of the big cat. Although some distance away the magic of the jungle brought the sound closer. My companion intended to shine his torch in the eyes of the tiger to hypnotize him, meanwhile the native boys fixed up a running noose made of rawhide. With a loud roar the bush parted and the enormous animal leapt with evil intent. The powerful beam incredibly stopped the tiger in his tracks, whereupon the natives slit its gizzard with scimitars, though not before the little house boy Sagu had had his head crushed by an enormous paw. By moving in front of us he had undoubtedly saved our lives. Sorrowfully we buried him and turned again for Bandung.

It was now February 1942 and I could not take in all that had happened, but, thinking of Stanley Holloway's 'Sam, Sam, pick up thee musket', I would dearly have loved one, no matter how antiquated. We traversed several ravines, swam across fast-running streams searching for transport, received cuts from rocks and undergrowth, and did not bless the people who had blown up the bridges.

After crossing a fever-ridden swamp we came to a clearing and unexpectedly confronted the railhead. It was intact but with no rolling stock apart from a plate-layers' gig on which we decided to propel ourselves the rest of the way if the track was clear. As it was currently beyond our strength we rested for a day to get our second wind. We knew we could not survive indefinitely without some medication, as least quinine for the malaria.

Conspicuous by their absence, the Dutch Military should have been patrolling in force if they hoped to defend Java from the Nips. On reaching the healthier mountainous area of our journey it was a delight to bathe in the mountain streams and especially to stand under a little waterfall.

A few miles out of Bandung we reached the mainland proper and were greeted by the Dutch who decided to escort us the rest of the way. The Superintendent was shown respect and told them I too was important. Our survival astonished them. Despite protestations from my friend I was marched off and interviewed by the Commandant, a gruff sort who disbelieved my story. After I had been locked up for twenty-four hours and interrogated, I was again before the Commandant who was satisfied with my credentials (had I been guilty I was for the barracudas in the lake).

My briefcase was returned intact and untampered with; they must have had x-ray eyes. My downfall had been to assume that they would not speak English and to speak in German. Politely shown the door, a staff car at my disposal, I drove off at great speed in the direction of HQ. Wanting to reach civilization, I was to be disappointed. Halfway up the mountainside I was stopped by the PBI (poor bloody infantry), but soon allowed to resume my journey.

As I rounded a sharp bend billows of smoke choked the air as massive bonfires burned official files and papers. My enquiries as to what was going on were met by 'mind your own damn business' from the Quartermaster, who wanted to know where I had come from. He informed me that the Commander-in-Chief had departed for Australia that morning leaving orders to destroy everything, the C-in-C being our old desert pal General Wavell.

Hastily returning to Dutch barracks in Bandung I found the same exercise underway with destruction all around including Bren guns still in their grease. Gathering as many as I could pile into the back of the car, I returned unchallenged to HQ.

A Warrant Officer and I carried out impromptu weapons training of the office staff, mustering natives with scimitars, and then waited through several nights for the arrival of the yellow peril.

7

CAPTURE

THE WAITING was monotonous so I moved on, stopping at Bandung to load as much petrol and supplies as I could carry. An Anglo-Indian sergeant, Duke, from the Indian Army accompanied me. He was cheerful and willing to help in any way. On our road to Tjilatjap we collected two non-combatant officers who had left HQ to make their own way to the coast, a Captain and a Lieutenant. Driving as far as possible into the mountains we met an Australian brigade who asked us to join them, but we preferred to fend for ourselves. We left the vehicle camouflaged and we continued up the mountain with backpacks to the Aussie encampment for our first good meal in ages.

A body of heavily armed men approached the encampment and in good English said that the Netherlands East Indies Government had declared a truce with Japan to save the civilian population. The terms of truce were that the Dutch should hand over the British, American and Allied troops which would mean their own troops would be given special consideration. Having listened to this proclamation in silence, we decided otherwise. It was a case of 'take or be taken' and the better trained troops got control. Disarming them with minimal bloodshed we forced them to lead us to their vehicles which, being perched on the edge of a ravine, were soon pushed over, while the distraught CO wept.

Believing we were better off on our own we left the Aussies

and, retrieving the staff car, set off in the pouring rain. The drops fell as big as your fist and the whole landscape became a quagmire. It was impractical to go on in such conditions and so we sheltered for the night in a foul-smelling hillside cave. The animal droppings being too much for the officers they decided to sleep in the vehicle while we stretched out our car-cramped limbs. I was rudely awakened by Duke to find that our gallant officers had deserted us and taken our vehicle. They couldn't have left us, surely, but as they had even sneaked into the cave for the weapons they would not be returning.

They had contemptibly left us to our fate. Aware of the outcome whichever way we went we also knew that the 'general offensive' was on, with burnt-out villages as evidence. Bombers and fighters came in waves. This part of Java was pure jungle, fit for only monkeys, so why waste so much ammunition on it?

Moving into the hinterland, our clothing in shreds, we never met a living soul. We lost all track of time. We drank from streams and lived on papaya and other wild fruits; we became immune to stings as to other irritations, including the multi-coloured snakes marked like an expensive pack of cards with aces and diamonds. We laughed and joked in our delirium and on reaching the ultimate ridge foolishly stood exposed overlooking the vast jungle. A Navyo peppered us with machine gun fire and Duke was hit. He died in my arms crying 'Mother'. I cried too. Hardly out of his twenties, it was a terrible waste of life. Desolately I rocked as I sat, and began singing a song for Duke:

> Back in childhood days, I can remember
> Loving caresses showered on me.
> Loving arms and eyes so sweet and tender,
> What was their meaning? Now I can see . . .
> One bright and guiding light

That taught me wrong from right
I found in my mother's eyes.
Those baby tales she told
That road all paved with gold
I found in my mother's eyes.
Just like a wandering sparrow,
One lonely soul –
I've walked the straight and narrow
To reach my goal.
God's gifts sent from above
A real unselfish love
I found in my mother's eyes.

Laying Duke to rest in the best hollow I could find, I covered his grave with wild flowers. Absorbed in thought, I sat down in a clearing and was immediately surrounded by yellow faces. They gestured to me to put my arms above my head and fired at my head and feet when I was slow to respond. Frozen with shock, I noticed they had large faces with matching grins exposing lots of gold teeth. One spoke haltingly in pidgin English and later told me they were Manchurian troops enlisted into the Japanese army. They had been fighting in China for ten years, and they felt sorry for a lonely soldier. They fed me some messy gruel seasoned with spices which made me feel sick.

After being on the move for two strenuous days we reached a town called Garoet where a lot of immaculate American prisoners walked around as if it were peacetime – the long awaited American Artillery who had presumably handed over their guns and equipment. There was a great freedom until the 'second line' troops took over. We were rounded up with rifle butts and bayonets were thrust into our backsides and stomachs.

We were beaten if we did not respond quickly enough owing

to language problems. We later learned that the Japanese officer had learnt his perfect English at Eton but he failed to present himself as an English gentleman.

We were marched all the way to Batavia, three to four hundred miles through country I had already crossed, with no desire to do so again even if I had transport. I thought it was an impossibility for me, but the Nips thought differently. I laid the blame for my predicament at the door of the Higher Echelon, regretting sending Churchill the eighteen-inch cigar from Batavia. I only knew our destination was again to be Batavia because the Nips could not pronounce the word – it sounded like 'Gratiaviaiah' – and they appeared as concerned as we were about the place. I grieved for what was to come, the clinging leeches and cuts from wild pineapple leaves with razor-sharp edges.

> Poets say our lives are like the rivers that flow
> They surely know true
> Everyone a different kind of stream so they say,
> All on our way too.
> Here a racing torrent met
> Dashing on too strong.
> Here's a peaceful rivulet
> Babbling along.
> I have been just like a weary river
> That keeps winding endlessly.
> Fate has been a cheerful giver
> To most everyone but me.
> Oh! How long it took me to learn
> Hope is strong and tides have to turn.
> But now I know that every weary river
> Some day meets the sea.

The blessed state of limbo helped me to endure the next few

years as whippings and beatings were administered with tedious regularity. Concern now centred on keeping clean; all those sanitary things once taken for granted, such as soap and razor blades, were non-existent now. In the old Cavalry days at Tidworth we were once confined to barracks and made to take the law into our own hands with one who could not keep himself clean. With this curtailment upon our liberty we lost no time. It was cold and frosty as we waited until midnight, then threw him into the horse trough.

Years later in Cairo I met him in the Military Police with gleaming Sam Browne, grateful for his lesson.

I remember little of the journey from Garoet to Batavia but eventually found myself in Gloddop Prison with released criminals in charge of us. Issued with huge batons, they used them to full advantage on the relics of a fighting force. Living at least seventy to a cell, prisoners died off like flies. Corpses were put onto the low roof coverings of the bungalow-type buildings to rot giving out the subsequent smells. Scant food was doled out over open drains intended for rainwater but now taking away excreta.

I tried to lift morale by organizing a concert and surprisingly the Commandant agreed. But we did not bargain with the Guards acting independently, who harassed us with metal thonged whips. It was off and on for a month until the Commandant decided he wanted to see it. I found consolation somewhere 'along the Rio Grande', thinking back to the Garrison Theatre, but the illusion was short lived.

We were to be kept weak on the orders of High Command in order to control and manage us. Logically, weak men cannot resist. Our one ambition, to get out of the death trap, was impossible in our state of rotting health. One young man wanted me to have his rice ration before he died, but he trailed off almost at once in my arms. Such a young face, he had no burial ceremony and we had not even knowledge of which corps he came from. It is strange and ugly to be conditioned to death but all feelings were deadened in the dung heap of humanity within the prison walls.

Some of us were removed as rebels to Tanjeon Priok, known as 'The White Man's Grave'. There were concentrated masses of barbed wire around us and we were overlooked by watch towers. We could at least see the light of day with no walls to hide it from us. The combination of irritation from fine sand,

3. Injections under the heart with a dirty needle. All ranks except officers.

heat and exposure aggravated by established tropical diseases developed multiple sores. Thankfully I was never encumbered by sores, for which there was no treatment; one could only sit in the sun.

When the devils held jurisdiction with wrongly directed energy into the most severe punishment, I learned from experience to be detached from the physical body. Unmelodious substitutes for living spoilt the melody of songs I sang to sustain me, as, cutting myself off from surrounding influences, I 'gathered lilacs down an English lane'. The overpowering feeling of isolation from civilization was, I knew, only the environment: the soul was not changed.

In our bemused state we did all manner of things, trying to build a chapel which was repeatedly knocked down by the Nips,

4. Java, Netherlands East Indies, 1941–2. This chapel was constructed out of rubbish by mutlilingual POWs at Tanjean Prison.

but we were determined to complete our task. At the very least we would have somewhere to worship and in due course we did prevail against the opposition.

5. While tied to posts, bamboo splinters were stuck under finger nails.

Swamped by thousands of cards to record rank, name and number and other private details, some of us banded together and put in names like Donald Duck, Mickey Mouse, Fred Astaire, Charlie Chaplin, and bingo numbers. It was difficult trying to invent names like Harry Syphilis. The exercise lasted several days before our captors, convinced they had the correct details, despatched them to Tokyo Headquarters.

Segregation into compounds allowed us to observe the activities of our compatriots in the camp at Tanjeon Priok. To relieve the Nips of the responsibility, commissioned ranks were put in charge of all POW rations. Intolerably, a handful of British officers misappropriated the rations into pasties for their own self indulgence and left none for the ranks who were slowly dying from malnutrition, tied to posts for misdemeanours they had not committed. Incapacitated officers fared no better from their brothers than the rest of us. One of their number had taken refuge in a paddy field and contracted ringworm. One could hardly put a pin between the sores. We bathed him in an old tin bath full of water, but had no other relief for him. The spread of disease was now manifest in the camp: principally typhoid, dysentery, beriberi and malaria.

8

THE DEATH HOUSE

FOR WHATEVER REASON I was singled out to go to the 'Chinese School' in Batavia. It was not a POW camp but was known as a 'Death House'. We were isolated, with no working parties, and were not permitted to converse. There was only one Dutch doctor, forbidden to practise, and medication was non-existent. Lying on cold dank tiles with no bedding, even the worst injured were required to raise their heads to acknowledge the appearance of the Japanese officers. Food was almost unobtainable, but the Javanese orderlies grew pea-shoots between wet sacking to cook and feed us. We occasionally had a mack-mack bird, otherwise no meat.

Most of the inmates were too ill to be aware, apart from a cheerful young Australian called Kevin. He had been blown up and impaled on the iron spikes of the bridge he was crossing in his jeep, his abdomen pierced from front to rear. He lay completely prostrate in one position all day. Permitted to stay with him to stuff his wounds with any old rags I could find, I fed him whenever there was anything edible to be found.

With fluid constantly running from me I was taken to the 'Death House' with dysentery and placed on a wire mesh like the kind used in rabbit hutches. From here I could see the Nips injecting water into the main arteries of a patient (supposedly to cleanse him). A half-inch pipe was inserted into the leg to speed

6. The death house in the Chinese School, Batavia, 1942. Not a POW camp.

death. In the staccato manner of the race I was told, 'This Censu. You injection tomorrow.'

During the night the Dutch doctor quietly crept in with a large bag and, kneeling beside me, prayed, then left. He returned with a boiling cauldron and made hot scalding tea with the contents of the bag. Although it appeared like tea (of which Java had abundance) it could have been made with the herbs he experimented with. He poured it down my throat all night and, miraculously, I was on my feet again in the morning. He disappeared and I deeply regretted not being able to thank him, for I never saw him again. I walked out of the 'Death House' to return to my charge, and was immediately beaten for escaping Censu. 'You fit man, you go to Nippon.' Having returned from death I was fit to go to the Land of the Rising Sun over three thousand miles away. Meanwhile I was returned to Tanjeon Priok with my entire wardrobe of a striped pyjama jacket and a mauve sarong.

A little white cow strayed into the compound. How, was a mystery. It was immediately surrounded by a pack of ravenous POWs. Not even a moo, it vanished, hide, flesh, bones and horns. Not one guard appeared to investigate the crowd. Presumably the Nips let it in as there was no gap in the fence. They are a curious people, almost cannibalistic in their instincts. I have seen them set traps for little sparrows which they consume raw, picked out of the trap and eaten alive. Such was the hunger of the prisoners, the poor defenceless undernourished cow stood no chance.

Everything moveable was being loaded onto ships in the Batavia docks for Japan. Huge bags of the staple rice diet, furniture and all manner of possessions were loaded by Javanese coolies and prisoners, by hand. Running up and down planks at a 45° angle, no concern was shown if a few dropped into the sea or died of fatigue. We spent long tedious shifts exposed to the midday sun.

The Javanese, though small, carried the huge sacks on their heads easily with no sign of fatigue on their blank faces. The prisoners took four men to carry each sack, to the amusement of the guards who gently persuaded with butt-ends of rifles and bayonets. Even with four to a sack progress was slow, and we contrived to reduce speed further without being too obvious.

Huge radio transmitting valves were being loaded into crates taller than a man, but with a hammer we reached through the openings and smashed each one. Luckily the guards, dozing in the heat of the day, did not detect us, as we knew the penalties.

Marching back to Tanjeon Priok, the little bags of sugar and flour secreted about us were found by the more alert camp

7. Dutch women thrashed for trying to give us bananas
on our way to the docks, Batavia, 1942.

guards. They scattered our loot over the roads, flogged the worst
culprits and further punished innocent and guilty *en bloc*.

At night it was so cold in the huts that we appealed to the
Commandant for fires. He agreed with an Oriental grin. Then
he sent the guards to find those responsible for 'this felonious
crime'. Termed a chief conspirator I was thrown into a punishment pit (used for even the smallest misdemeanour). It seemed
like an eternity without water where I sweated it out, though
there was in fact no sweat for I was frozen. My face and lips
swollen, I could only grunt: 'I am with You always.' If He was,
why leave me to perish in this way? The moss on the walls lived,
and would continue. In the blue sky I could see through the grill
above me; birds soared, there was life out there.

My mother taught me, 'prayers can only be answered if they are prayed,' and I sought communication with God to sustain me. I visualized the chapel we formed from rubbish despite all opposition. Mustiness, mildew and the smell of my body excretions suffocated, but I learned to live in other compartments of my being. Strange feelings of restrictions giving way assailed me: I was floating on air, rid of all the pain and anguish. To say a thing 'must be', is the power that makes it so, for my prayers were answered, and my soul rejoiced in freedom as I surveyed myself below.

Freezing water stirred me to wakefulness: no escape from man, the cancer of the earth and I was part of that pollution. I screamed and waited for whatever. Hands dragged me into the blinding sunlight where I struggled rebelliously and violently. If I was to go it would be flag flying; these bastards would not win this war of attrition. I was no hero but would not yield to tyranny and shouted the one word they detested, 'Churchill!' There were blows upon my back and in my fury I thought they were crucifying me.

Realization dawned that 'they' were fellow prisoners for I heard guttural English; they were Dutch. I recognized the voice of Jack Laundman as he pummelled me back to the land of the living. Putrid tasting liquid was poured over my raw tongue and down my sore throat; wet and warm as it was I gulped it down.

When I began to recover I thought I had been through a bad nightmare. I did not know how long it took. Instead of rags I wore a dirty dark-green paper-thin suit with the number Atchi-du-Atchi (88) on the left breast. I was shod with flat pieces of board elevated with two-inch square pieces of wood. Cotton strapping lined with straw fitted between the big toes and across each side of this uncomfortable platform. This footwear, in general use, was slipped off when entering a hut. Only bare feet were allowed on straw *tatami* mats in 'billets'. Later we were issued with the cloth rubber-soled boots as used by the Nippon army. Also split-toed, I assume they were used for climbing trees which were all these monkeys were fit for.

Bodies had to be dealt with before our journey and I was one of those detailed to help carry them over three miles for cremation. Placed in orange boxes atop a pyre of wood on a piece of spare ground, there was no funeral service except for our feeble, 'God be with you; ashes to ashes and dust to dust.' Anguish consumed me as I reflected upon the culmination of the Java tragedy.

The Gunners

I'll tell a story of Java,
'Tis not gallant, brave or fair,
Just a story of a handful of men,
And the sorry mistake made there.

Of a few British lads, good Gunners
To Infantry converted in haste.
Never before had they done this job.
It seemed such a pitiful waste.

Belgium, Egypt, Italy, Singapore,
Their job they had always well done,
But this story begins in Sumatra
When they were ordered to spike their gun.

As they came to the Isle of Java
With retreating fed up to the teeth
They swore they'd have no more palaver
Their weapons were not made to sheath.

AN ENGLISHMAN'S PEACE AND WAR

The Colonel ordered a big parade,
And with these words he said,
'Gunners, I'm sorry we have no guns
Good Infantry you'll be instead.'

No murmur came from that parade,
In their hearts they grieved the more
'Twas like taking a sailor off his ship,
To put him to work on shore.

Late one night came the order to move,
To a 'drome away by the sea,
Not many thought that night would prove
Their last on earth to be.

All night long the bombardment went on,
Dulling ears with terrific din,
Yet not a word were these men told
That the enemy had managed to get in.

Trench mortar machine-gun rattle
Seemed scarcely a mile away,
Yet none were told to prepare for battle,
That was a mistake I say.

At exactly 10.10 that morning,
The unit fell in on parade,
Yet still no news was given them
Of a landing the Japs had made.

'Away to your billets,' the Sergeant said,
'Your kit in your bags quickly cram,
I really don't know a thing as yet,
But I think we are in a jam.'

As we moved off at the crossroads,
Enemy tanks came rumbling along,
Spewing cannon and gunfire from their load
To the leading lorry they swung.

Forever I'll hear one Gunner's cry
In anguish: 'For God's sake, stop.'
Already a shell had struck his leg,
And the next, in death saw him drop.

Not many from that shambles escaped,
Except just a fortunate few,
Who like myself missed being draped,
By the reaper in sombre hue.

So fate decreed that I was there,
I am bound by that fate to say,
I must have been spared, to declare,
Precious lives were 'thrown away'.

These men achieved no great glory,
But from a soldier's point of view,
They have their place in the Empire's story
Of duties MEN DIED TO DO.

9

THE *SINGAPORE MARU*

WE LEFT for the Land of the Rising Sun in open boats. My last sight of Java was a giant iguana chained by the neck to the dock wall of the harbour. To me it represented the utmost cruelty. The boat was crammed to overflowing with human misery, but I felt no sympathy. These were the ruling sahibs who had lived in Singapore on a good colonial wicket, aping the gentry at the expense of the British tax-payer while keeping the natives down. They were victims of their own corrupt stupidity. These were the 'Raj' and, apart from the Afrikaners, the most spoilt, detestable people on earth. Even in the hands of the enemy they were still spoilt and selfish, not lifting a finger to help their own dying. I made no friends on that long arduous, uncomfortable journey, and did not rate highly the chances of survival for my compatriots.

We landed at the docks with the usual omissions: no food, water, or privacy to relieve ourselves. Prodded into line, a Japanese Lieutenant announced we were to be cleansed and prepared for Japan. We could not have guessed what this entailed. First we were paraded through the streets of Singapore before local Malays, Chinese and others, then handed over to the Sikh guards who had gone over to the enemy. Still in possession of their British .303 rifles, they did not hesitate to train them upon us or use them for an occasional dig with the butt.

Lined up in rows and made to bend over, white-coated

Japanese soldiers tested us for dysentery, much to the amusement of the locals. Ragged and starving (many injured by the rough handling at the hands of the Japanese soldiers), now the Sikhs were allowed their vengeance for centuries of British Rule and hate. To efface this humiliation I thought of Rudyard Kipling's 'If'.

> . . . Or watch the things you gave your life to, broken,
> And stoop and build 'em up with worn out tools . . .
> If you can force your heart and nerve and sinew,
> To serve your turn long after they are gone,
> And so hold on when there is nothing in you
> Except the Will which says to them: 'Hold On!' . . .

Conditions at Changi Prison were indescribable but we were

8. The acid sheep bath, Singapore, 1942.

not incarcerated there. For us, there was 'no room at the inn'. We were returned to the docks and were treated to an acid sheep dip to cleanse us for our trip to Japan. In bitter anguish I inwardly called on the Lord with all the strength in my being: 'I have kept Your commandments, why should I be condemned to this hell on earth?' To my astonishment I heard a voice answering, 'Quite so, thou hast kept My Commandments but thou has not learned to love or care.'

I thought of the lonely Lieutenant 'T' whom we had left on a log in the jungle. He dared not go back and dared not go forward so we had left him to his fate. I remembered the Dutch women thrashed and insulted by the Japanese guards for trying to help us on our way to the docks, and the intolerance I felt for the ex-ruling Sahibs now sharing our fate. I struggled to detach myself from the physical indignities thrust upon me, and the words of St John 13.34 came to mind: 'A new command- ment I give unto you that ye love one another.' How could we love these enemies, hosing us down with fire-hoses, taking the top off our skins after our acid-bath?

Transferred to the filthiest ship I had ever seen (an old British tub which must have sold for scrap in the year dot) we had no time to look around though I keenly sought a glimpse of any lifeboats. There were two on the port side with daylight showing through the bottom. I sighted the shipbuilder's name, it looked like 'John Brown of the Clyde'.

The initiation to Cavalry discipline which I had regarded as military injustice in the thirties seemed far away now but was proved good grounding for our present dilemma with the Japs.

The only Cavalryman in that ill-fated company, I felt remote as we were herded like cattle onto the filthy, good ship *Singapore Maru*. All sense of time was lost. An emaciated young lad turned and said, 'I have had enough,' and threw himself headlong down the ship's hold. I had not the strength to hold onto the arm I had grabbed. Our destination was the same, down among the ballast with hardly any air to breathe and nowhere to lie except on one's side in pools of sweat.

The hold was divided into three tiers and we were housed on the bottom before the third tier, with no hope of survival if hit; water was already leaking through the plates. We were allowed two at a time to the toilets on the top deck, but as few had strength to climb the ladder, the stench was indescribable. It was a miracle we did not suffocate; galley slaves could not have fared worse. In the darkness of half-light we sensed whether it was dawn or sunset.

When men died up to fifteen at a time, the bodies were passed hand to hand to the top deck. When the Nips decided they did not like the smell they summoned about half a dozen from our hold to the deck. We were brought to attention with blows from rifle-butts, while a dysentery- and disease-ridden padre (from another hold) strove to give some kind of burial service to the corpses laid among the food we were destined to consume.

On our way to Bangkok through the South China Seas the *Maru* seemed to go one yard forward and two back. Too ill to be seasick, we prayed for a torpedo to end it all, as she continuously rolled. But no torpedo came; how could the US Navy overlook such an easy unescorted target? Perhaps it would be better when we reached French Indo-China.

A British Commanding Officer who had been keeping a low profile eventually found his way to the bridge for an interview with the Captain. Pleading bitterly on our behalf that 'the ship was not fit for pigs', he was clapped in irons for his 'insulting insinuations' — he was never seen or heard of again.

An American-Japanese called Goto once paid us a visit at great risk (I well remember his smart grey lounge suit). Caught in

Japan while on holiday from America, he had been declared unfit for military duty because of his age and had been recruited as an interpreter. He concluded, 'I am grieved for your conditions and there is nothing I can do for you.' He left a half-bottle of whisky and some aspirins as he climbed back up the ladder. Too fatigued to shout 'thank you', I was glad someone would benefit from his gifts.

As we pulled into Bangkok harbour several of us were ordered on deck to clear the ship up and dispose of the recent dead. Stewards waiting on the Jap Officers with sirloin steaks dashed back and forth from the galley. One steward fell flat on his face on the deck we had just hosed. Precious steaks were everywhere followed by a mad scramble from the prisoners. I did not partake but received a rifle-butt in the stomach. Others were beaten unmercifully. Order restored, steaks were gathered up and taken to the Officers' Mess smothered in British blood.

Indo-China was still occupied by the French as one of their territories, and the small French tugs chugging around the bay flying the tricolor came in close to us. Seeing prisoners on our ship, they came in closer still to jeer. We turned our backs and asked to be returned to our hell-holes.

Underway again, the same terrible seas confronted the worn-out frame of the *Maru*. She almost seemed to turn over. I tried to count our blessings but could find none as, dragged up onto the deck one by one to stand in the brutal gale until our limbs froze, we waited for the Captain's important announcement. An eternity later he strutted onto the bridge and announced that we were to be given 'a demonstration of the might of the Nippon nation'. Our attention was directed to a cannon roped to the stern of the ship. The gun crew in position, an out-of-tune bugler sounded his battle call, and the Japanese stood rigidly to attention. Immaculate in his uniform, the Captain raised his arm and gave the command to fire. His voice was carried away in the gale and the crew charged the antiquated gun which gave a dismal shudder (likewise the ship) and a feeble shell popped like a pea into the sea. Stretching to full five feet nothing, in broken English he said that we were to have 'the great privilege of a military funeral on reaching Formosa.' This we 'earned' by paying respect to the Japanese flag in the ceremony we had just witnessed. My swollen tongue was already out with scurvy and would not retract back into my mouth. This had been a rehearsal for our forthcoming military funeral.

One of the guards mentioned Taman and I knew we would not touch land again until we reached Formosa, now the independant Republic of Taiwan, some 3,200 miles from Singapore. The route we took via Bangkok had lengthened the journey, for which the old ship with its human cargo was never equipped. There would be a further thousand miles after Formosa (in straight lines) though our course was zig-zag; we could have been travelling to the moon for each mile seemed like a hundred. Putting my trust in faith and hope for relief, my prayers were answered. I was seized and taken on deck (anything was better than the dark hell among the ballast). Remember 'Old Bill' in Flanders Field and his catch phrase, 'If you know a better 'ole get to it.'

I was dragged rather than walking to the filthy galley. With gesticulations it was made clear that I had to scrub it and get rid of any rubbish. The galley was not fresh but was like mountain air to me and I decided to make it last if the guards would let me. The hope of getting some extra food did not materialize. I was watched to make sure I neither ate nor secreted anything under my sparse clothing and was roughed up from time to time in a search. Allowed to go to the stern to empty pails of slush I discovered the Nips urinated into them so was not tempted to

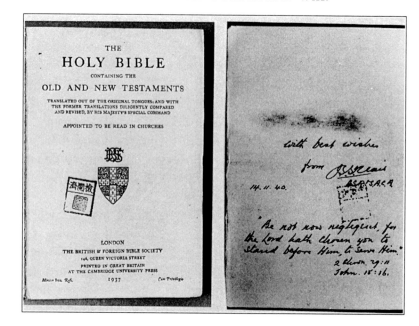

9. Japanese military censor stamp on the fly-leaf of a small Bible given to me under fire by a Scripture reader in Tobruk, Libya, 14 November 1940. Confiscated in Japan, it was returned to me several weeks later.

eat. The contents of the emptied pails were immediately consumed by sharks who followed the ship from the southern hemisphere into these cold waters and waited as usual for our dead.

Bleeding again with dysentery, I contaminated the Nips' food and hoped they would all come down with the disease. The sharks never had such a good larder, but my own belly-button was touching my backbone.

Working through the night I became preoccupied with memories of the recent past. My only possessions were a blue Gillette razor-blade and a small Bible (with the Jap censor stamp on the fly leaf) given to me under fire by a Scripture reader in Tobruk. Before leaving Java I had had two rings, one a memento from North Africa and the other given by Kevin at the Chinese School to trade for food which did not materialize. I was mortified when the Japs ripped them off my fingers (I still bear the bayonet scars) but it grieved me that I was afforded no opportunity to return to Kevin with the news that we no longer had any collateral. Not permitted jewellery, the Japanese love to put gold on their teeth, as did the guards and the Manchurians who captured me.

Like the rest I had been through the furnace and tempered. The more difficult it became the closer I felt to God. I hoped the price of past indiscretions had been paid and determined to live to reach Formosa. Sensitive to the suffering of colleagues in captivity, those fallen in conflict were also very much in mind as conflicting thoughts sought expression:

The Fool

'But it isn't playing the game,' he said,
And he slammed his books away,
'The Latin and Greek I've got in my head
Will do for a duller day.
'Rubbish,' I cried, 'the bugle's call,
isn't for the lads from school.'
D'ye think he'd listen?
Oh, no, not at all. So I
called him 'A fool, a fool.'

Now, there's his dog by his empty bed,
And the flute he used to play,
And his favourite bat –
But Dick, he's dead

73

Somewhere in Java they say.
Dick with his rapture of song and sun,
Dick of the yellow hair,
Dick whose life had but begun,
Carrion-cold, out there.

Look at his prizes all in a row:
Surely a hint of fame!
Now he's finished with nothing to show,
Doesn't it seem a shame?
Look from the window!
All you see, was to be his one day,
Forest and furrow,
Home, and now
He goes and chucks it away.

Chucks it away to die in the dark.
Somebody saw his fall,
Part of him mud,
Part of him blood,
The rest of him, not at all.
And yet I'll bet he was never afraid
And he went as the best of 'em go,
His hand clenched on his broken blade,
Slain by the formidable foe.

And I'd called him a 'fool',
How blind was I,
And the cup of my grief's abrim,
Will the glory of England ever die,
So long as we've lads like him?
So long as we've fond and fearless fools,
Who spurning fortune and fame

Turn out with the rallying of their schools,
Just bent on playing the game.

A fool! ah no!
He was more than wise,
His was the proudest part,
He died with the glory of faith in his eyes
And the glory of love in his heart.
And though there's never a grave to tell,
Nor a cross to mark his fall,
Thank God! We knew that he battled well,
In the Last Great Game of all.

He was an exemplar of the many whose lives were forfeit in conflicts to protect our freedom and the values we cherish; I am honoured to have known Dick as a very dear friend, but he would not have wished to be rated as any different from the rest of us.

— 10 —

BURIAL AT SEA

THE *Maru* edged its way through the straits of Formosa to the main harbour of Taman. In our unkempt dilapidation we lined the decks, jeered at by onlookers as, half-naked, we concealed our anger and frustrations. Our dead lay on the deck while arrangements were made for burial. The wait took us to the end of endurance; many fainted and the rest of us swayed with the wind.

Boxes similar to orange boxes appeared, into which the dead were thrown, some face down, with limbs dangling over the sides. Stiffened limbs were broken to get them into the 'coffins'. Guards lounging on rifles raised the butts if anyone sagged or moved his feet. The coffins, nailed and battened down, were loaded into a huge rope-sling ready to be hoisted at a given signal to the dockside by the stevedores.

The gun was swivelled round to face the open sea, and with the stage set the Captain and minions with expressionless faces stood rigidly to attention. The untuneful bugle call was sounded, the small cannon fired and its slow moving shell dropped harmlessly into the sea. The Captain saluted and the flag of the Rising Sun was slowly lowered as the signal was given. The stevedores hoisted the sling and immediately the boxes opened exposing their contents to the blazing sun. That was the end of our military funeral for the dead.

Immediately, we were forcefully herded to our quarters in the

76

bowels of the ship. Already more than overcrowded an extra deck was to be installed directly above us to accommodate several Japanese Army units returning home. Army engineers moved in to erect sleeping platforms with the occupants below bearing the brunt of the colossal fall of debris. The platform was built around the sides of the upper hold and across, leaving an aperture in the centre without which we would have suffocated.

Our route to the latrines was blocked and with no other way of passing these troops, crowded to the bulwarks, it was every man for himself. We were plagued with rats, lice, bugs, cockroaches and some crickets whose shrill chirrup was a constant reminder of days in the tropics. The rats were tame, nibbling at toes as we lay in a semi-comatose state.

Jack Fiddler and Cliff Walker, my immediate companions, lay dead either side of me. I had promised to see their relatives if I survived, which seemed most unlikely. I still keep their addresses.

With a thousand miles or more to travel until we reached our final resting place, the *Maru* pitched and tossed even more with the extra load. We lived on the aroma of food served to the new passengers who were travelling first class compared to our squalid surroundings.

The old ship began to leak more water and we thought we would either drown or be suffocated in the sludge. Conditions got so bad we had to be taken aloft, exposing us to the cold Manchurian wind. Instead of heat we now had freezing temperatures and had to go below again. Owing to many deaths we could now lie down and we became impervious to smells from sweat and rotting bodies.

As we neared Japan the message filtered through that we must be prepared to meet our honourable captors on the mainland of Nippon. Shadows of men, we were dragged, almost carried, from the bowels of our hell-hole and assembled on deck for a lecture on victorious Japan.

Tongues swollen from scurvy lolling out of our mouths, our rags rotted with sweat, the cold winds blew and bit through us, while some of our dead still lay among the sparse raw vegetables. Lined up to face the bridge, waiting for the almighty Commander to appear, excreta slurry expelled from our bodies slid down matchstick legs to the deck. Many of us were bleeding profusely.

The Imperial Guard, our captors, aimed blows at will. If hell existed we had found it. Senses heightened by starvation, I missed little of what went on. The ship suddenly manoeuvred into the gale, hurling us to the deck in confusion. Hitting the bulwark, I looked over the side at what appeared to be a huge sea-serpent with rough scales. I flung myself back towards the unseaworthy life rafts and wanted to cry but had no tears, for beneath the heap of fallen bodies men died from lack of strength. The guards took this opportunity to pounce with rifle-butts, enraged by our disrespect for our captors. For two hours we stood in that biting wind, skin too thin to show goose pimples, but still no Commandant.

A lone silhouette against the angry sky, the mysterious padre stood, emaciated beyond recognition with dysentery and the fatal black death known as summer diarrhoea, but we had no summer here. Immediately, the guards felled him. I never knew his name and never saw him again.

Eventually the Commandant and his lackey appeared on the bridge. The interpreter was not present and I wondered if his freedom had been curtailed because of his brief charity to us.

Unceremoniously lined up with heads bowed to the Emperor of the Rising Sun of Nippon, we were addressed in pidgin English:

'British dogs, you must prepare your filthy selves to be presented to the glorious victorious people of Nippon. I do not have to remind you that you are not guests, and you will work hard towards the glorious day of our victory.' He paused to let this sink into our stupid minds. 'Your destination will be Kyushu, where you will await further orders before dispersal to other camps. You will not eat until you arrive there. It is good to keep you hungry and then you will appreciate my kindness during this voyage. I learned of your ways at what you call the world's most famous Military College, Sandhurst, so you will see that I am not and will not be fooled by your devious ways, neither will the great Nippon nation. Obey my faithful guards and you will not suffer. Should you choose to disobey they have my orders to dispose of you after you have suffered the penalty of your disobedience. Please accept my kindness and theirs. You will now return to your quarters and prepare your miserable selves for the days to come, and you will assure me "My will be done". You will be paraded to observe what progress has been achieved, if any, and if there is none, you will pay, according to the orders of our Imperial Emperor which shall be death to all who disobey.'

Left to the mercy of the guards as he strutted away, we were herded once more like cattle to the bowels of the *Singapore Maru*. I lay on my side in a stupor; the man next to me had passed on. I questioned myself aloud, 'What is the objective, carting us all this way to die?' The voice I had heard before answered, loud and clear, 'You are going to live through all of this, do not despair.' I did not think to question that ethereal voice but of one thing I was certain: it did not come from anyone in the hold.

I had not enjoyed the luxury of a wash since leaving Singapore when we had gone through the sheep dip, all of six thousand miles away. I watched the cockroaches creep over my dead comrade. Then came the rats. At dawn we were herded on deck to see if there was any improvement in our appearance; we were then returned to the hold. Without soap and water we could do nothing. In the Western Desert I promised myself never to waste another drop of water, but now I did not have a drop to waste.

With a kick in my back I was dragged up on deck by two guards and taken to the apology for latrines. I had to clean them. At least I would be left alone until I had finished for they could not stand the stench themselves. With buckets of sea water and my hands I began, knowing whatever I did would be faulted and I would be beaten. In Java they had got us to cut the grass around Gloddop Prison with blunt bamboo sticks, and having failed we were beaten till we could not stand. My morale did not break then and it would not now.

Proud to be British with skin now like rawhide that could withstand their beatings, I silently sang, 'Rule Britannia, Britons never, never shall be slaves', which was a laugh for that was exactly what I now was. Abandoned in the desert and in the Southern Hemisphere, as were the rest of the small group with whom I was affiliated, I was completely cut off from my comrades. Pausing on the deck with the wind roaring about me, I witnessed the finger-nails being ripped off a defaulter and felt choked. I had to live to expose all of this but such total horror, cruelty, deprivation, filth and starvation are not easy to convey to paper.

St Matthew 10:38 – 'Fear not them which kill the body, but are not able to kill the soul: but rather fear Him which is able to destroy both body and soul in hell.'

We stopped at Okinawa Gunto in the East China Sea where there had been a tidal wave (called a *tsunami*). They are not connected with the tides, and travel up to five hundred miles an hour. Most of the ships lay on their sides in the harbour, but although the *Maru* creaked, moaned and groaned, she held together, which must be a recommendation for British workmanship.

Here we took on more Nippon troops. Perhaps we would drift into the Pacific and be found by American submarines, but it was a faint hope.

A leaky hose pipe was rigged up with which we were sprayed from time to time, eliciting wide gold-glinting grins of satisfaction from the Japs. The salt water on running sores caused great pain but helped to cleanse the wounds. Twice daily we continued to drag the dead up on deck, getting covered in excreta in the struggle. Towards the end of our voyage things improved, as we were allowed more escorted visits on deck for longer periods, to watch the might of the imperial Nippon forces at firing practice, deadly serious when firing that little cannon.

PART THREE

THE CAMP

ER HUMAN CARGO having been discharged on the rickety
quay at Kita-Kyushu, the *Maru* pulled away, her siren a
plaintive sigh, while I watched with a feeling of insecurity. In
the dusk, with lit torches, our new guards were silent. They had
no rifles, but an assortment of whips, spears and bamboo sticks.
They did not appear to be young men and some were minus
arms or had only stumps. Perhaps they were veterans of the war
with China and Japan.

Standing in our rags the Manchurian wind blew across and
through us, spray from the inland sea soaking stunned and
paralysed bodies. Numbed limbs cried out for exercise. We were
transferred to the damp holds of coal barges which were like
Chinese junks. As they were half full of coal (mainly dust) it was
difficult to breathe.

After a seeming eternity there was a minor collision, and
about six of us were dragged onto the filthy deck to tie the barge
to its moorings. In a strong tide with the swell running it was
not easy to hold the narrow inadequate boards in position. Well
below the quay, the landing planks were almost vertical.

With frozen hands and feet, endurance waning, I looked up
and saw shooting stars (I knew it to be astigmatism). Confused,
I felt myself falling, biting through my lip as I went. I knew I
had hit the water and that this experience was not new to me.
I remembered floating on a piece of driftwood with a lady, and

in a semi-conscious state found solace in the stars flashing around me as I sought to throw off the stupor.

I was rolled over onto my back and a light was shone into my eyes. The tears came and the mist cleared as someone slapped my face with vigour. A yellow face was thrust into mine and once again the blood surged through my veins. I felt beneath me: I was on a rough straw mat; the slapping went on, and hot liquid was poured into me by a beautiful girl but she had a yellow face. I wondered what was happening. Then I saw Sam's face; he shouted, 'Come round, you idiot, you fell in the drink,' and I heard him mention grappling hooks. I sat up, realizing this was not the barge. Was it the camp and how had I got here?

When I recovered, Sam explained that the Nips had slung me over a pit pony but why they had fished me out of the sea was a mystery. I was lucky to be alive. Jesus wants me for a sunbeam, but not just yet. The miracle of life is so precious that I could not understand why we were so anxious to snuff it out. I had hoped and prayed that the 'quality of mercy is not strained'. I hoped it was not lost in this storm which enveloped the world and not of our making. 'God is love' and love had been destroyed in this century. Our experiences were, to say the least, violent and gory. It occurred to me that this might be a propaganda camp (as the Germans had) and we might be lucky enough to end up with some flesh to cover our bones.

While with our semi-soldier guards, they did their best on meagre means to make us comfortable. The diet was mainly seaweed, octopus, sweet potato tops, polished rice and pickled *dykan*. We were allowed to bathe in the village communal bath and slept on hard *tatami* mats. We had shelves for our non-existent belongings. Rats as big as cats raced around these shelves at night, the fleas were plentiful if we reached under the thin blankets we had been given, although on the whole we were comfortable after the hell-ship and the barges. Some semblance to civilized beings was achieved.

In the first few days the Nips allowed some of their young girls into the camp. They had not been told about us and were at a loss when confronted by a large group of bedraggled Europeans. They gestured from their eyebrows to their mouths to indicate the difference between our big noses and their flat ones, a feature which seemed to amuse them. They could not have had much contact with the outside world. In multi-coloured kimonos, with paper-yellow skin and apple-blossom cheeks they were all Madame Butterflies and I was grateful for the splash of colour. We were served by them in a makeshift but clean dining hall. One took my eye but we were not allowed to converse alone. I sought possible ways of escape but knew it to be futile in this land of slant eyes and flat faces.

Within two weeks we were brought back to reality with a jerk. The Army arrived to take us from the transit camp. The little Japanese girl smiled sadly but dared not wave goodbye. The saying, 'East is east and west is west and never the twain shall meet', is not true, for there was a great attraction between us.

Our new Commandant swaggered up to our bedraggled group and in broken English said, 'Remember you are the enemy. Our great leader Tojo has commanded the Army to treat you as prisoners of His Imperial Majesty, the Divine Leader, Long Live Hirohito San. You are the first to reach Nippon and you must make a good impression. You are commanded to remember that you are not guests, and the people of this place will be punished for treating you as such.'

Prodded into line we were faced towards a disabled Nip wielding an open cut-throat razor. He had a stump for a left arm and a crafty grin on his face. My mother's willow-pattern dinner service came to mind and I knew it was never intended to be like this. First in the queue for the Head Ripping Ceremony, I slowly made my way towards the bizarre distorted figure waving the razor about. I was pushed onto a stool, the stump was placed on my forehead and the Nip said 'Atchi-du-Atchi Dami,' meaning 'eighty-eight, no good.' Sitting taut, my hair was ripped off taking with it every known and unknown parasitic insect. It was a new experience to be bald for the first time, but not a trivial event, for every occurrence was momentous to us. Some of the lads, fearing worse things, fought against it and had their fingernails torn off by regular Army troops.

Those who had been our hosts watched, expressionless, awaiting our departure, delayed while the punishments were meted out. Lined up for the long march ahead we had no idea of the distance to be covered as we left the little fishing village for Tako in Hiroshima, carrying our sick with us. Humming the National Anthem as we marched, I received a slap across the face but bracing my shoulders in the best Army tradition, defiantly murmured, 'God save our Gracious King, Long live our Noble King!'

A two-day march took us to Tako with prevailing conditions deteriorating all the while. Our new Commander, Osaka Chui, addressed us from the guardhouse, but the exact wording would be difficult to repeat precisely. 'You know you are not guests of the Great Nippon People, but you will observe the laws of the Japanese Army. You are prisoners and if you do not obey you will be punished according to your crime. There is a Geneva Convention which says you are to be treated as Nippon soldiers.' His voice went up and down an octave. 'You will sign to say you have been fairly treated at all times as the Geneva Convention states, and that you have had all the benefits of the Nippon Army, including excellent food . . .' and so the harangue went on.

When we had returned to our huts the guards lost no time going around with papers for signature, which included a written threat that if we did not sign we would march fifty kilometres without food or water. I did not rate our chances of doing even five kilometres before the strongest would begin to collapse. NOT ONE MAN SIGNED THAT PAPER.

Crude farm carts arrived pulled by water buffalo (we called them yaks). The guards climbed onto the yaks, leaving us to hobble as threatened. We received no food or drink to start our journey, nor would we.

Parasite-infested by day and night, there was no hygiene or sanitary arrangements. The mass of small insects that live on the skin tormented us. Crabs, lice, fleas and the parasites of scabies carrying dangerous germs, the fleas with plague, and the lice with typhus. Another pest was the mosquito, causing malaria and the dreaded yellow fever. I wondered if we would ever fit in with Western civilisation again. At least I had no sexual diseases to contend with. Venereal disease among some of the men was rampant before their capture so they bore additional problems. The Nips were not immune in this direction and as far as I could gather the penalty for them was death.

There had been no treatment for such conditions in Java, so the little devils went to a doctor who was a prisoner and demanded help. The only drugs he had were a few aspirins which he gave sparingly in return for some extra rice. They must have discovered his duplicity for he suddenly disappeared.

Men now struggled along on improvised crutches. Beri-beri and boils were rampant. I wished in my heart that I was back with the Phantom Brigade, expected to live off our own resources, behind enemy lines with miles of desert sands, the occasional mirage, purple-hued swaying palms, minarets and the oasis. They looked so real, if only I could reach out and touch them. I never wish to kill or maim anyone. The universal custom was all wrong.

Reality was the crack of rifle bullets. Two of our party, unable to stand the torment any longer, had made an attempt to escape by throwing themselves into the paddy-fields that were on either side of the track. It was a token gesture, perhaps to end it all. They lay half-submerged in the water, but the coolies (probably Koreans) never lifted their heads. They had just seen two men shot in the back; although foreigners, they surely must have felt some emotion. I stumbled out of line, crawled into the ditch and turned the bodies over. The guard shouted, 'Kurra Nanni Ka' and I knew I was for the high jump, so pretended to faint and slid into the murky paddy-field water. Although I only touched the bodies my hands and rags were saturated and needed cleaning off.

With a rifle-butt in my back I was pummelled by the first of the guards. They could not grab me by the hair as I had none. They pointed to the bodies but as I could not drag them out single-handed, I shook my head. They could not strike me down for I was already down, though not out for the count, and strangely they accepted my efforts to help my comrades. I was offered a cigarette by one of the guards but refused, indicating it be given to someone else, but the guards turned away in disgust.

Dragged to my feet, I was pushed with several others to recover the bodies. We were then forced to kneel on the dusty rough-hewn road, heads bowed and arms outstretched before us, to await the return of a small party from the nearest village.

A flagrant disregard had been shown for the orders of the Imperial Emperor Hirohito: 'Prisoners must not try to escape.' One of the bodies exuded an unbearable stench, obviously gangrene, and the Nips donned white cotton half-masks across their noses. Meanwhile the coolies were waved to the side of the road and encouraged to pelt us with anything that came to hand. Significantly they chose soft clay rather than pieces of rubble on the track. Their life must have been a dreadful existence, but I would gladly have exchanged places with them at that moment.

The small party returned from the village carrying rolls of hessian and some sacking. They ripped off two lengths then remembered our tortuous position. Those who had not fainted struggled to now bleeding feet caked in mud.

I was one of two called to the front and given a sailmaker's needle, which the guards produced, to sew the corpses cocoon-like into the sackcloth. I just wanted to lie there and rot but a whip struck me across my back. The sewing complete and slings made, a half-a-dozen of us were loaded like camels to carry the dead.

We had now covered about twenty-five kilometres and the Jap Commandant had been as good as his word: no food or water for fifty kilometres because we would not sign his wretched document. On reaching a plateau we set the death bundles down, to gather bracken for a funeral pyre. When ignited the guards stood us to watch in the heat and smoke until the very last ember died away. I felt I must close the door on this vulture – death.

The guards led us to an unhedged field full of *dykan* which was covered in 'benjo' (Japanese for excreta). Starving men will eat almost anything apart from human flesh and we threw ourselves down and tore at the roots. How could man walk away from all this with a balanced mind?

Insensitive to our surroundings, hobbling kilometre after kilometre, we had circumvolved the plateau. We looked up and saw the hillside was covered in a mass of beautiful cherry-blossom; the pink hues beneath a gorgeous blue sky was magnificent to my tired eyes and faith rushed back to fill me with hope as I noticed what appeared to be a wooden shrine with ornate roof (possibly of the ancient Shinto religion). This preoccupation with religion was a welcome distraction from the circumstances in which I was submerged.

At last our punishment trek was at an end as men collapsed to the ground. Others in silent mortification were dragged unceremoniously and shuffled into line. A roll-call was ordered and with croaked voices we responded – Itchi, Nee, San, See, Go, Rocko, Sichi, Atchi, Que, Due and so on, but of course many numbers had fallen on the way.

Expressionless, our new Commandant surveyed us. 'You have come to this camp to work hard. The Japanese people are merciful and understanding. If you do as commanded according to Military Law you will receive a just reward. If you disobey you can be punished by death according to the Geneva Convention. I learned to obey in your country.' (Many of their officers had been trained in England prior to the war.) In good English he continued, 'You will rest for ten days at the end of which you will work ten-hour shifts in the mines, and if you work well you may even have a cigarette or two. We are a generous people, you will be fed well according to your ability to work. All ranks will obey and work. If you defy you will be punished like a Japanese soldier.' Tediously he went on and on. Could he not see we were in a state of collapse and what about his marvellous food? 'Please God lead me to it.'

Night was falling fast when at last we were led to a grubby dining hall. The meal, such as it was, consisted of awful pickled horse-radish and one small scoop of rice. The other vegetable, like ivy leaves, I learned later was sweet potato tops.

One of the prisoners had been a Naval Dietician, and called an 'extraordinary meeting' without first obtaining permission from the Camp Commandant. He was supported by a ship's engineer, captured while his ship was in dry dock, a fine figure of a man in spite of suffering like the rest of us, with a bushy greying beard. A Scot by birth, with a swaying gait, he was a great inspiration, at least to me, as a father figure. We gathered around to hear the discourse on diet and the news was not very comforting. The bare minimum should be no less than 800 calories and we must have roughage. He had saved the 'intended ration' from his meal and demonstrated with some improvised scales and scoops. Underground workers in the mines were to receive a mere 450 calories a day, surface workers 220 calories. There was no food for the sick so we would be giving part of our ration to them, reducing intake still further. There was no heat-producing capacity in the food we had received to combat conditions underground. He stressed emphatically that on this diet our life expectancy would be eighteen months. His forecast was subsequently proven.

The Commandant must have had radar for he appeared with a guard. The Dietician was stripped and flogged and the next day frog-marched out of camp. Ordered to kneel down and bow our heads in shame (for what was surely no crime) our meagre rice ration was burnt. We occupied ourselves by trying to bring together a choir in what was left of our promised ten days' rest, making the best of what we did not have.

12

THE MINE

O UT OF CAMP for our first encounter with the Pit, it was a pleasant distraction to see some of the civilian population *en route*. Their little homes were fragile and the women carried their youngest babies strapped to their backs, but predominantly had one young child on each hand and one in front, as yet unborn. They were not much better off than ourselves but seemed to be breeding well on their handful of rice and seaweed.

There appeared to be a lot of imported Korean labour, large and angular, whose wives, with large breasts exposed, would run out to mimic us, pointing at our noses. We christened the area 'Tit Alley'.

In a sea of some three thousand small islands, the Japanese mainland was composed of fluid volcanic matter and this was evidenced by tremendous seepage in the subterranean depths resulting in very poor quality coal. Air pressure called for the combined effort of four men to open and close huge doors, when a foul smell blew from either direction. Water dripped everywhere as we struggled through slime to the coal-face which was invariably about eighteen inches low. At the entrance to our designated coal-face the pit-props were halved and quartered. Crawling through large 'rat' holes, dim lights attached to hessian-made mining caps had to be discarded and pushed through in front of us, along with our *binto* boxes which held two small scoops of rice and a bit of pickle for the ten-hour shift (but no water).

The lengths to be excavated were marked up with whitewash each day by the *shokos* (pit deputies) before we commenced. The three metres of coal per man was carried to the surface by conveyor belt and pit tubs drawn by ponies (fed solely on sawdust). I felt like Orpheus in the Underworld but at least we were away from the reach of the torturing bastards. Injuries occurred every day, cuts and bruises, lost toes or fingers. Men would not cover their backs in the heat and many were scored with wounds which became embedded with coal dust, causing gangrene to raise its ugly head again. Pit batteries were always undercharged so we usually came out in total darkness or, with luck, an odd lamp burning, often carrying the injured on our raw backs. At times when the coal could not be reached, the *shokos* placed dynamite shots to loosen the coal seams, clearing the coal-faces of all personnel before lighting the fuses. This was done by means of a whistle which was blown from the safe end. Invariably it came too late and we had to make a run for it.

Once, overcome by fumes, I passed out. Unconscious in the total darkness I would have been blown to smithereens but for Smudger from Liverpool who, at great risk to himself, returned to rouse me and drag me to safety only minutes before the charges exploded.

There were a few miners among us, some from a Welsh Artillery Battery. Without their advice we would have perished underground. One who helped me considerably had his back broken. He had previously confided the deep love between him and his wife which had fortified him in these dark days. When we eventually got him back to camp, I was touched when, just before he died, he asked me to sing 'Land of my Fathers' for him and 'Bird Songs at Eventide' for his beloved wife.

Unkempt and filthy on our return to camp, we cleaned ourselves in a concrete communal bath. Small and round, heated by a furnace beneath it, there were usually scum, germs and crabs floating on top, but if we were lucky, the water used shift after shift was hot. We then had our two bowls of rice, some sweet potato tops and perhaps a little delicacy like octopus or blushing fish, a tropical fish which looked very tempting but turned one's face tomato colour and made the heart thump.

Casualties in the pit could have been avoided but no safety precautions existed. While making our way to the surface, the pit tubs on long steel hausers or cables were often let loose. When the ratchet holding them was released, they hurtled down without warning at about fifty miles an hour. One of our lads walking along the tracks was crushed between the stationary truck and one of these oncoming tubs. He sustained fifteen fractures but held out until he was released, then died.

By now I was suffering from emphysema, abnormal swelling caused by pressure of air or gas in tissue especially of the lungs. I also had dry beri-beri characterized by paralysis and difficult breathing, with action upon and through the skin.

We had a doctor with us, a United States Naval man, but without drugs he resorted to recommending men for light duties. Constant beatings did not deter him, but his black hair turned white. One of the few allowed to retain his hair, the change was patently obvious. He recommended me for light work. To heat the boiler for the miners' grubby bath, I humped timber which was wet and difficult to ignite. Much effort and struggle ended in failure and my 220 calories were withdrawn, so I was reduced to living on any rubbish the guards threw out.

At this time there was an occurrence which infuriated me. The International Red Cross delivered drugs to the camp. They were handed to the US doctor in their presence, but were confiscated the moment the Representatives left, and raised hopes fled.

One day Goto, a guard noted for his bad temper, made straight for me with his whole bearing spiteful. Nishimura, on duty in the guardroom, saw his intention, and stepped in his path. I had never seen a guard intervene to assist a prisoner and was grateful for the streak of humanity. Goto knocked him to the ground but Nishimura picked up a trestle-form used by the guards and hit Goto over the head. I did not stay to see more, but next day on parade for an early roll-call I saw Nishimura in the shelter of the guardroom having his breakfast. It was a live sparrow he had ensnared, and with blood running down his chin he consumed the lot including the feathers.

Called to the front I was ordered to join the relief shift. My light working ration of 220 calories a day was then restored. As we left camp a very heavy steel bar with a piece of metal welded at the end was placed in my hand. From the outset I was devoid of strength but carried this thing to the mine and, collecting my lamp, followed the shift through the mud and slime to the coal-face.

With gestures towards a moving belt a *shoko* demonstrated the use of my bar. I was to rake out the coal from under the belt and load it back onto the belt, all the way up from the base to the top. It was no mean task, usually done by Korean women who seemed to have vanished. I was to do this task unsupervised. With no prodding guards, after eight hours I had worked my way to the top and now had my *binto*. It had tasted good.

Intent on sabotage, I reflected on an incident involving a Scot. A guard had poked his rifle through the billet window to molest him and the Scot had grabbed the rifle, but was pulled out through the rice-paper window. It was two months before we saw him again, when two of us carried him from the pen to the billet. He was raving mad with feet swollen like footballs. Eventually he came round to grunt, rather than speak, but made it clear he had been beaten every day, and buckets of freezing water had constantly been thrown under him on the wooden floor so he could not lie down.

As I made my way to the pit exit, memories filled me with anger and I changed my course. The belt was split into sections, and the coal, when not in tubs, came down a series of chutes onto the belts at various stages. The belt then diverted about a kilometre from the coal-face to come through a special construction like a small tunnel built of concrete blocks. It was well lit, dry and went to the surface, but prisoners were never allowed to use it.

I followed the route to the surface, and on arrival, with a lot of luck, I found the main generator. Being on my own I crept to the dynamo and shoved my rake into the spindle of the coil. It almost took me with it as the long steel handle wrapped itself like a bit of putty around the dynamo shaft.

Shouting was everywhere but so was total darkness. Putting as much distance as possible between me and the machinery, I joined the guard, a prayer on my lips that if discovered the rest of the camp would not be punished. In the confusion it was not noticed that I no longer carried my steel rake. I was not challenged and resolved to keep my own council, even from my trusted comrade, Jack Laundman the Dutchman.

The pit was idle for at least two days, giving the prisoners a well earned rest with little or no interference from the guards. Fortunately there were no reprisals. It is possible that a Korean or even one of themselves was suspected, for we had seen civilian Japanese sustain a beating outside the mine office just for arriving five minutes late for work.

On our journey to and from the mine we passed a school, and I was fascinated by the small schoolchildren. Little tots in kimonos, with bobbed black hair, hundreds of them shuffled in perfect formation into the school, leaving their clogs outside. If we passed them at leaving time, they streamed out, each finding his or her own clogs without hesitation. One day I spotted a little blond head. No-one else showed any interest in that little head but to me it meant a lot, for there must have been an infiltration even into that community.

It happened during the night. The awful tremor, then our huts fell off the concrete blocks on which they loosely stood. With visions of falling into a volcanic fissure I did not want to be swallowed under the surface of the earth. The eruption came from a mountain overlooking Kobe, roughly 140 miles east of Hiroshima, and we felt the heat. It was frightening and un-nerving as chaos reigned. Shortly after this incident I was able to speak to Scottie, the ship's engineer who had supported the Naval dietician. He still had his beard, looking every inch the old sea salt and had managed to retain his Merchant Navy hat-badge, his proudest possession.

He now related the horrific night of terror when a former eruption at Kobe had resulted in his presence among us. He had fled with the population to the sea to escape the huge wave of white-hot lava, burning all and everything in its path, flimsy houses and foliage. House-sized sparks flying in the sky were the sole illumination. Ash shot fifty miles into the air and the sound of the explosion was heard three thousand miles away.

Scottie had made it to his American cargo vessel, the USS *Playboy*, plying between Honolulu and the Japanese mainland with mixed cargoes of bamboo, timber, rice and machinery. He did not know how they managed to get up steam into open water to shelter at Kid Suido, and then make port of Shikoku Island. Many of the ship's crew had perished in the white hot lava, and all but one of the officers were missing. He was the survivor, but as the ship's engineer he could not take on the responsibility of the bridge. Unaware of the death blow to Pearl Harbour they put to sea, hoping other vessels would come to their assistance.

A coded message informed them that America was now at war with the Axis, and then without warning the Nips boarded the ship from a flotilla of Naval vessels, manhandling them to the mainland, and blasted the ship out of the water with the ship's pets still on board. It was out of the frying pan into the fire with a vengeance.

As he concluded I remembered the words of the Director of the American aircraft firm Kitty Hawk: 'The American Nation has no sentiment for the British and are out to exploit them to make a fast buck.' 'Lease-lend' was then in operation but their tanks and planes were inferior products. I knew this as one of the unfortunates who had used them in place of our own worn-out equipment.

With no rainbows on the horizon we decided to organize a concert. Scottie, myself and one or two others chose Robin Hood and his Merry Men. I drew the short straw as Maid Marion, but also got to be musical director minus instruments. With normal daily chores to do, it was almost an impossible task to get a cast together. We received no assistance and although we had permission the guards disrupted rehearsal just as in Gloddop Prison, Batavia. They appeared with whips bearing metal thongs and plans were temporarily abandoned.

After an interval the Commandant intervened; he wanted to see some Western entertainment. I formed a small choir of about six volunteers: few could sing in tune but we managed with a Welsh bass-baritone who always sang off-key loud enough to drown the others, with myself as tenor conductor. Having no music we sang easy rhythms and whipped the tempo of some Irish songs.

The Japanese officers in the front sat stony-faced throughout our pathetic little concert, but at the end of it the performers were ceremoniously given a cigarette when we would most have welcomed an extra ration of rice.

It was a brave show as the participants were all very sick men. In for a penny in for a pound, we sang the National Anthem. Rising to their feet the whole camp sang and cheered. It was heart-warming as straining hearts poured out such wealth of feeling in defiant song. In face of such impromptu national fervour the Commandant and his henchmen beat a hasty retreat. When put to the test, inborn national pride of the British can never be discounted.

The prelude to a stupifying drama occurred in the early hours one morning. The Commandant stood on his rostrum to meet the second shift. As they arrived a fusilier, Trooper D., was dragged from the ranks. Stronger than most, he was very thick-set. Apparently, leaving the mine ahead of his shift he had climbed onto the pithead office roof, torn down the flag of the Rising Sun and paraded in circles with the flag draped around him on the Nips' physical training ground. He continuously issued words of contempt: 'Down with Tojo, down with Hirohito, spit on their evil guts.' This was far removed from the 'hail fellow well met' we all knew and admired.

The Commandant in halting English referred to the Geneva Convention. Trying to escape was one of the most punishable offences, but flagrant disrespect for the flag of an enemy was the greatest crime of all. He could not find words to express his anger and, adamant that the insult was punishable by death, did not doubt that there were accomplices who would share the same fate when caught. Without trial, D. was sentenced to be shot at the next sunrise.

Next morning we were herded outside our bug hutches and while D. was brought onto the parade ground trussed up like a chicken, an interpreter was rushed into the camp. A court was convened and the interpreter read out the charge:

He could commit hara-kiri according to Japanese military law that his soul might eventually reach its haven of rest with his forefathers. (D. was a Catholic and suicide would have damned him) or he could be beheaded by the Commandant's own sword (but D. would not be bound to the stake prepared for this doubtful honour; nor would he be blindfold). The choice was made and he set an example not one of us could hope to emulate. He did not sob or call on the Virgin Mary as the bugle gave an out-of-tune call to arms; he just laughed. Rifles were raised, then cracked like a whiplash, and Trooper Dursley lay there in a heap. Driven round the bend by the Japs themselves, perhaps it was a happy release.

Warned not to touch the body for two days, those not on shift had to cleanse themselves then were led out of the camp and up to the Shinto shrine past the cherry-blossom trees on the rough mountain path. We were to kneel in neat lines with bowed heads in silent supplication to the Shinto God for some time before the Commandant arrived.

Colonel Petrie kneeling beside me muttered that he refused to bow his head to their heathen god. I advised him to bow it or have it chopped off. Glancing at the dangling sword on the alert Yamamoto who stood close by, he nodded and bowed his head.

Two days after the execution I was called to the guardroom, expecting another beating. I was wrong. I was given a cigarette

10. Kneeling with weights upon hands until collapse. This was a common occurrence in all prison camps where I was held. Usually bricks were placed on outstretched hands while kneeling; the prisoner was then left for endless hours until he collapsed.

and it was made clear that I had to remove the corpse from the vicinity of the guardroom. I could appreciate the urgency for the stench was shocking. In rigor mortis the body was a twisted mess, and if death had not been instantaneous he would have bled to death from the terrible wounds.

Calling for volunteers we had to break an arm and a leg to straighten the body in some coarse canvas sacking over which the guard poured kerosene. We were ordered to cover him with foot-lengths of tinder to make a neat pyre which the guard ignited. On unconsecrated ground with a small tattered Bible I uttered a prayer. The flames spiralled towards heaven and we stood transfixed as the guard poked at the ashes. As noted on many other occasions, they had no respect at all for the dead. With great sadness in my heart I fled to my billet.

Around this time a small cyst appeared near the joint of my left wrist and although unable to use my left arm I was not excused from work in the mine. Short of men for the shift, neither the hours worked nor the amount to be extracted were reduced which was a mammoth task for sick men on a diet of rice, seaweed and sweet potato tops. With no surgical instruments the cyst could not be incised but the American doctor said he would smite it when I returned from the mine the next morning. In great agony, that night I slipped in the filthy slush and fell, knocking my wrist awkwardly with tremendous force against a timber. With a surge of pain the cyst disappeared and the use of my arm, although painful, slowly returned.

13

SAGA OF THE PIGLETS

IT WAS TIME for celebration. The Commandant informed those on morning roll-call that we were to have our own meat: some pigs would be delivered to the camp in the next few days. The gift was bestowed upon us for our good work, on condition we fed them well, bringing them swiftly to maturity and bred them so that he, his brave guards and ourselves could be well fed to build up our strength for the difficult days ahead. Those not required would be handed to the civilian population.

Some of the men on 'light work' were detailed to construct pig-sties (a formidable task). With crude tools the timbers were hacked from tree trunks by hand. Like the pit-props it easily splintered; we called it 'bugger-me wood', but the sties were completed in three days. Expecting some fine stock we were soon disillusioned when, on the fourth day, all the camp were summoned on parade to witness the handing over of 'this wonderful gift' – six piglets slim as greyhounds with the impossible demand that they be fed on our 'left-overs'. In God's name, our ration was little enough.

It was made clear that the pig-keeping would be done by the sick, while the rest of the camp carried on with the coal-mining stints. After a few days we requested more food and without a blink the Commandant said he 'would give our petition serious consideration'. The food arrived in the form of fish roes.

As we proceeded to cook them in a rice cauldron the smell

attracted a Dutchman. They were not allowed in our quarters. Having fought the Dutch before leaving Java we had no reason to trust them. To curry favour, they became despicable tale-tellers, with the exception of Jack Laundman. My only opportunity to speak with him was over a bowl of rice at mealtimes when he voiced his shame of his compatriots. The intruder kicked over our cauldron. We grabbed him angrily by the neck, but he struggled to tell us, 'Try them out on the pigs first.' Eventually we agreed and when sufficiently cooled we fed the roes to the pigs. It is a mystery how the guard failed to observe us but the Dutchman's intervention was timely, for the next morning the pigs were all 'stiffs'.

Dragged out to face the wrath of the Commandant and his Lieutenants, we received slaps on the face before being made to kneel with bare knees on the gravel for a considerable time. When the Commandant addressed us his fury and anger were unbelievable. Yamamoto was the worst as he strutted about with his sword dangling between his short little legs. Bullied beyond endurance, we were ordered to carry the pigs to the front of the guardroom. This incident was of grave importance to us for 'small numbers' were now responsible for the 'punishment of innocents' not involved with the crime. The outcome was an order to eat the pigs raw. Every man refused which resulted in a decision from the Commandant – a burial party. This was done with ceremony at the side of the guardroom, not less than six feet deep. The grave diggers were the handful of braves who had fed the fish roes to the pigs.

Trying to keep a close watch on events and progress of the war in Europe, I made my way, on several occasions after nightfall, to the Commandant's office next to the guardroom. Luckily for me, I was not caught. I got a certain thrill from these nocturnal escapades. The Commandant left his Japanese newspapers

11. Propaganda photograph of the author in Japanese uniform, 1942.

lying around and, taking the odd printed map from his file, I followed the war in Europe almost to its conclusion, especially the fall of Berlin.

A certain dignitary was to visit the camp and shifts were cancelled as all areas had to be spruced up; even the walls of the stockade had to be scrubbed to look almost like newly-planed timber. At night our hands were raw, our limbs ached and we fell into our billets with exhaustion. The days were long and we yearned for the mine to get away from the camp and the guards; even the very sick were made to work.

A makeshift hospital was rigged up – a false illusion of medical attention. Japanese army uniforms were brought into the camp for each of us and a new pair of real leather boots. A special meal was to be given to us and if we gave our full co-operation we would receive more privileges. Drugs were brought in and handed to the American doctor. Many sacks of rice, sweet potatoes and tubs of pickled *dykan* were put on show with sides of meat and British Red Cross parcels. It was a galaxy of food we were forbidden to touch. Crates of saké (rice wine) came next and cigarettes in little green packets which were imitation Woodbines. If this was to be the order of the day we would want for nothing. 'We must be on our best behaviour at all times as photographers would be present.' Our minds boggled: all this food yet our meagre rations had never been increased despite our appeals for the sick. The Commandant was the hardest of men.

Told we could write home, or should I say 'cross out', we were handed preprinted postcards, each bearing four sentences which read:

> Dear Wife the weather is fine and so am I.
> Dear Mother the Japanese are kindly people and I am very well.
> There is nothing to worry about my health is good.
> I am not sick, remember that I am being well looked after by the great Nippon nation.
>
> Your loving ———-

Only one pen was allowed per billet so it was a laborious business to complete the cards, and many were reluctant when they saw the sentences. I guessed it was only propaganda and they would never reach home, so I crossed out all the sentences and signed with a rude word the Nips would not understand, and I did not care if they did. The belligerent guards softened a little and gave me some tomato plants. Using improvised rough boxes I planted them between the barrack blocks.

The great day arrived and as there was no intention of placating the Japanese High Command we held a war council. It was however decided that discretion was the better part of valour. We would put on a show that even their guards could not match, and perhaps the Nips would relent and let us have the meat rations after all.

The high ranking Officer arrived in a military vehicle from

12. Propaganda photograph: a galaxy of food.

which he stepped with jackboots resplendantly polished, his khaki uniform like the British. He wore gold epaulettes, red tabbed lapels and rows of medal ribbons, Nazi-style peaked hat, kid gloves and riding crop plus a Sam Browne. Tall for a Japanese, if he had worn a British cap he could have been taken for a British Officer.

Standing to attention in the front row I saw his German Iron Cross with the Nazi swastika in the centre of it and knew we could expect no mercy from this man. His faceless retinue were of the same ilk as they strutted behind him. We had agreed to show them our spirit was not broken, and it was a credit that despite all, our men had not forgotten their British Army training as they marched with military precision.

The visitor inspected the whole camp, then announced that

the prisoners should assemble in the main hall where trestle tables had been erected. It was hard to believe the galaxy of food laid out was for POWs. Plates and bowls were ready, also tomatoes, tangerines, oranges, apples and several other fruits, neatly arranged pyramid fashion in the centre of the long tables. There were two bread rolls per man and a drink in front of each plate, but there was no sign of any cooking. We had to remove caps and be seated, then we waited in silent anticipation.

The scene was set, cigarettes were lit when the cameras flashed, and we were immediately rushed from the scene of plenty without a morsel being touched.

The visit appeared to be going well until the Jap Quarter-Master reached the empty pig-sties. He had issued the orders for us to have livestock (there was plenty in the billets if he cared to look). He roared angrily, thrashing his jackboot vigorously with his crop. Under double-guard, I and a few others involved with various things in running the camp were detailed to follow the retinue around for the inspection. From the conversation it appeared that all camps had been instructed to keep livestock of some kind to supply its own meat ration.

The red face of the visitor turned purple as the Commandant tried to placate his ravings with an explanation regarding the disappearance of our livestock.

Outside a world war raged, yet here we had two high-ranking officers wrangling over six little pigs. Although the arrangement must have been governed by their economy, the incident sardonically amused me. Our small escort was brought to attention outside the office where they held court. Raised voices bore out an inexplicable trait of Japanese character – to humiliate one another in public.

We had a long wait as the verbal battle dragged on. Finally the higher echelon reappeared and the camp was assembled to hear the verdict, preceded by an abusive tirade against our villainy. 'For killing piglets without consent we must expect extreme punishment. We must consume the dead pigs, this was the order of the High Command; we should exhume the animals forthwith.'

From the ranks, absolute silence. Not one man moved. Continuing to arraign us, the Commandant motioned for a spokesman to come forward but no-one obliged. The Nips wanted reaction, some protest, but they got nothing so the guards were ordered to hustle us but it made no difference; no-one would dig up the pigs. Such stubbornness after so much suffering was remarkable.

As we stood, an order was issued and all the goodies, which we had eyed with longing, were withdrawn. All was dismantled, drugs snatched from the doctor; we were stripped of our new uniforms and boots which were loaded up and taken out of the camp. The exception was the Red Cross parcels which were stored but not issued until a much later date.

The final reprisal was the withdrawal of water for two weeks; there was no way out of this one and the mine created tremendous thirsts. The shifts were to be extended under close observation by the *shokos*. The doctor's appeal on behalf of the sick was ineffectual. I don't know what happened to the pigs nor do I care but I hoped some would be consumed by the bully boys, and kill them.

Air raids began to plague us. Making no attempt to avoid flak, brown-coloured planes without the usual camouflage and with no distinct markings flew at high altitudes dropping their loads on the industrial parts of the city. Several were shot down. They had no fighter escort so must have flown very long distances. We only knew they were coming because the Nip guard scurried for cover leaving us standing. They must have been warned for no siren was sounded. Later, fighter planes dropped rough pieces of wood with chalked messages on them.

Being so dehydrated we were glad to go to the mines to suck moisture from the mud. Too weak to walk the hundred or so spiral steps, we asked to use the walk-in tunnel. The mine was heaven compared to the surface, now the raids had started. Huts were destroyed outside the camp. We were not sign-marked as a Red Cross Hospital or a POW camp but international law was ignored by the Japanese. We often saw empty Red Cross boxes marked 'British' but never USA or other nationalities. Promised a visit from the Swiss representative, we still waited.

We shuffled back off night shift rather than marched and then normally received our ration, but one morning it was different. Instead of the usual abuse we were returned in total silence by a subdued guard. Strangers were present in scruffy Japanese uniforms with pikes. They looked too old for service life. The regular guard were drawn up with full kit and the Commandant stood to attention with his back to the troops. Many orders and drill movements later, they left the camp forever. Three times they shouted '*Banzai*' for victory, then they were gone and I whispered a prayer of good riddance.

A new Commandant addressed us but there was no introduction to the guard who prodded us back to the billet and their mindless destruction (my tomato plants trodden into the ground). Unfed, we lay down to sleep in despair. The next day we were informed that the Red Cross parcels which had been stored in the camp were to be released. Perhaps life would be bearable under the new guard. The old guard had gone to war; we hoped they would rot and decay in some far-off jungle.

An air raid was in progress as we were shepherded into the

13. The death tunnel.

tunnel in the camp. In this makeshift shelter there were ventilation shafts like small chimneys. We had no suspicions of the guards' intention, then in total darkness a liquid smelling like paraffin dripped in. As it touched me I knew it was kerosene. I knew then that the war must be almost at an end as the use of the tunnel became clear. The yellow devils meant to fry us like pigs.

We struggled to the mouth of the tunnel to be met by machine-gun and rifle-fire. At least six fell wounded or dying. With no escape I fell with them and others fell on top of me. My last memory was a mysterious white figure standing with right hand held high between us and the firing line. A great weight on top of me compressed my lungs and I passed out.

With misted vision I recognized Jack Laundman bending over me, doing his best to clean me off. He gave me some pungent liquid to drink and I began to recover. Only the British had been taken to the shelter. No one had been allowed near the tunnel for some hours, when the dead and injured were removed.

The killing was a reprisal for the raids that had killed many civilians. The Commandant was old and reluctant to carry out the order from Tojo, but disobedience would have meant he and his guard would have been killed, so they used their killer instinct but it did not explain the use of kerosene.

In this camp the British had always born the brunt of punishment; more self-disciplined prisoners, we were the most hated. I suspect this was motivated from fear. Instinctively the Japs knew they could not beat us, and at every opportunity we threw the name 'Churchill' at them and they replied 'Churchill *censu*' – 'Churchill dead.'

14

GUEST OF THE HEAD SHOKO

A CALL for Atchi-du-Atchi rang around the camp. I hopefully ignored it, but I was frog-marched to the guardroom and sluiced down with a hose pipe. Dressed in the loose robe with short wide sleeves as worn by both sexes in Japan, I felt quite a charlie. I was escorted to the main gate and marched out of the camp to the private quarters of the head *shoko*. I was very suspicious and hoped my exit had been seen by some of the other prisoners. The guard dismissed, I was shown into the main living room by the lady of the house who wore a brightly coloured kimono with a wide body-band drawn tightly around the middle with a bow at the back. I was motioned to sit cross-legged opposite the master of the house, who clapped his hands and said a prayer, much as we say grace.

A combination of nature worship and ancestor worship, Shintoism has no known founders, fixed doctrine or scripture, with its divinities called *kami*, varying in nature from personified natural phenomena to deified persons. These factors expound the Oriental mind, and some of the finer points lay behind the reasoning of my hosts to whom Shintoism came before family and friends. This is why girl babies were often drowned at birth. It was an honour to father a son but the opposite for a girl. If directed by their priests to slaughter us all, it would be done.

Colourful flags and bunting were flying above the house. It was obvious a celebration was taking place. Gifts of fish and other edibles were brought in by friends and relatives and hung on lines beneath the eaves to dry in the sun.

The *shoko* had been presented with a son but I had no gift to offer. The invitation to his house had been imprudent but approved by camp authorities. I wondered how to get some of that food back to the camp. With pride the *shoko* inflated his chest and beckoned for the baby to be brought in for inspection and precariously passed around from one to another. I looked on with unease. Shaking his head with vigour my host pointed to the lady of the house and then to the baby and in practised English announced, 'Wifee number two Atchi-du-Atchi', and waited for my approving nod. He clapped his hands and Wifee number one appeared in picturesque dress with immaculate raven-black hair drawn back Madame Butterfly style. The tea ceremony to create peace of mind to performer and partaker was about to begin; it was simple and graceful.

Hours had passed since I arrived and I began to wonder if I had been forgotten, for I had missed my precious rice and needed the *benjo* place. The room was sparse but tasteful with few Japanese trinkets. An *abashi* charcoal fire in a large earthenware bowl burned in the centre of the chimneyless room.

My host silently scrutinised me as he smoked a long, thin metal and bamboo pipe with a tiny bowl. I was glad of the pipe and small ball of his light-coloured woolly-type tobacco passed to me, for prior to this I had been shaken by a demonstration with his curved veteran's army sword carried in a leather sheath. He had withdrawn it from the scabbard and had me feel the razor-sharp edge, then unexpectedly with a yell of '*Banzai*' had raised it above his head and brought it down on the *tatami* mat in front of me. He then returned to his meditation, constantly filling the tiny bowl of his pipe.

Rising to his feet he beckoned me to follow him into the

garden, the lady of the house close behind as we stepped under a ginkgo tree in its maturity of which my host was very proud, with its fan-shaped leaves, yellow flowers and fruit like apricots containing edible nuts. Considered sacred it is usually planted near to Shinto temples. The *shoko* was an enthusiast in this garden representing nature with subtle sophistication in limited space. It was spiritual food to my starved soul after so long within prison walls. To me this was the willow pattern of enchantment.

The lady of the house had roasted a liberal number of the edible nuts from the ginkgo tree and tied them securely in a silk scarf around my waist under my kimono. My host had either not thought of the consequences of them being found or he had passed the word to the guards. I was not even searched on my return to camp and the men were so glad of the nuts they did not reproach me for my day as a guest of the enemy. As far as I know I was the only prisoner to be invited out of the camp.

Accorded Japanese courtesy on a momentous day in their lives and escorted back by guards with expressionless faces, the sight of a new born babe was reassuring, a message of renewed hope from God. I was returned to reality with the kick of a mule and the bestiality of man.

A fussy little man from the International Red Cross arrived in a brown pin-striped suit and trilby. He was refused an inspection of the camp but permitted to see a senior officer. The Gunners' CO, Colonel Petrie, volunteered. To assist and support him, several less senior ranks were allowed to accompany him. We determined to report the regular beatings and worse that occurred in the camp at Hiroshima, long shifts in the mines on starvation diet and the lack of suitable clothing or footwear.

But our spokesman was silenced (the Nips had so much to hide, not conforming to Agreements and worst of all no respect for the living or dead). How could we tell all to Doctor Paru-Ve-Cheni? But the doctor was no fool and through an interpreter ordered the immediate release of our parcels (only partly complied with).

Presentation of our circumstances was not going to be permitted. However, from beneath his jacket the CO produced a sheet of grubby paper which was quickly placed in the briefcase before our visitor was hastened out of the camp. Where the paper came from was a matter of conjecture.

At the end of the war I enquired the whereabouts of Doctor Paru-Ve-Cheni and was told by a Japanese doctor at Wakayama that he had died of starvation in a Japanese POW camp just outside Tokyo. This was confirmed at the Imperial Palace in Tokyo. They had ensured that the report from our CO could never reach his superiors.

A sequel at the camp after the Red Cross visit was equally sadistic. No words could convey the suffering experienced throughout the Far East for which I wished our tormentors would roast in hell. No nation should be forgiven for such heinous, despicable crimes!

Colonel Petrie was marched to an empty billet to be punished for passing the paper to the Red Cross representative. Under armed guard with fixed bayonets, he was kept on his knees on the *tatami* mat of roughly woven straw which bit into his knees. This continued for a month. We tried to rush the place to our cost and the rescue had to be abandoned; it was foolish but we had to try.

Finally dragged out of camp, his ashen face and bleeding knees haunted me. He had sacrificed himself for his men. About two weeks later his clothes were handed over to us. It was not difficult to imagine his fate, for the same ritual had been carried out at Tanjeon Priok, Java, when some RAF men on a working party jumped a plane, started the engine but forgot the chocks. They were executed on the spot but their scant possessions were returned to us at the camp. I was desolate and rebellious. Jack Laundman was no longer allowed to visit me by his compatriots for fear of reprisals on them by the Nips.

Another horrific occurrence was in the pipeline. It was night and my visit to the *benjo* hut was a forbidden exercise. As I passed 'the cage' there was rustling, but no other sound could be heard in the camp. All the guards snoozed on the bench where they sat on duty. *Benjo* places were compartments separated by doors over which one could see. There were no seats so one straddled the gully. Always liquid, it had to be scooped out each day by the sick and put on the vegetables to encourage growth on an infertile land of lava sparsely coated with soil.

Creeping along the cat-walk with a wary eye on peculiar insects I heard a faint gurgle from a stall. Grabbing the door open I found a POW with a broken knife-blade honed razor sharp pressed against his throat. I snatched the knife away and I dragged him out. I should have thrown it away but kept it which landed me in a lot of trouble later. (Daily searches, even under the floorboards, were made.) He gabbled incoherently but acquired powerful strength and we wrestled until I had to knock him out. If I left him he might die and if the Nips found him he would certainly die.

Bitterly cold, the wind bit as I left him propped against the wall of the *benjo* house while I crawled to the doctor's billet. Luckily I was not caught but had difficulty in rousing the doctor to explain my call. His immediate reaction was to let the Nips find the man, but crawling back to the POW I was closely followed by the doctor who must have had second thoughts.

Our friend was still unconscious but breathing; lifting him, we put his arms round our shoulders and prayed he would stay silent. Owing to lack of stamina we had to drop him, but we lay either side of him to give him warmth as we could not carry him any further. I hoped I would not be missed.

We awakened early as day was breaking to find our friend had somehow recovered and left. There was a disturbance at the guardroom and we hoped he was not the cause of it. This distraction did however allow me to get back to my own billet undetected, then came the call for Atchi-du-Atchi.

Rubbing my eyes as if just waking I made my way to the assembly point opposite the guardroom. Three guards held the POW face down in the earth. Whimpering like a puppy and still blood-clotted, he had completely lost his marbles and I feared discovery of my involvement. The doctor was pleading with the guard. His rugby tackle had failed to prevent the POW in his frenzy from antagonising the guard, who would not release him until a senior officer arrived. I feared it would be the pig Yamamoto.

Eventually the Commandant strutted in and, leering at us, ordered the release of the POW who immediately attacked and kicked the guard. With bulging unseeing eyes, saliva dripping from his mouth, he then spat and kicked the Commandant. The sight he presented filled me with humiliation and disgust.

A promising lad, reduced to the state of self-slaughter, now lay spread-eagled with a Jap standing on each outstretched hand while another stood at his head with a pike to his throat. The whole camp was assembled and our new guard, more brutal than the regulars, appeared, carrying the traditional Japanese pillow to place under the head of our compatriot, while the guard Commander emerged with a club like the bludgeon used in medieval times.

Jack ~ Laundman ~

Unexpectedly, the more kindly but rarely seen Tanaka San appeared (ranked equivalent to a Major) and, going straight to the guard holding the club, took it away from him. Then he and the Commandant went into the office. The assembly grew restless waiting; no one had eaten that morning. The doctor was beckoned into the office as we prepared for another long wait. They all emerged looking grim.

The Major addressed us in his broken English. 'The victorious Nippon nation are a merciful people but do not excuse violence of the kind you have witnessed upon your Commandant. The only punishment is death but we have not decided how it will be carried out.' With that the parade was dismissed. Our friend was dragged into the cells behind the guardhouse and I was returned to the billet under guard.

Nothing happened for several hours and no food was brought to me. The punishment did not fit the crime but it is impossible for us to understand the Oriental mind. We were all open to persecution if we ran into a bad tempered guard.

Allowed to collect my few pathetic possessions I sat waiting for the arrival of the Nippon guard. I did not know of the decision reached in the guardhouse and still thought that I had been called because of my involvement with the prisoner.

The guard arrived and escorted me to the huge ominous gates that had to be manhandled open. 'Death before Dishonour', the Regimental motto of the Death & Glory Boys to whom I had been seconded, seemed more fitting than my own *Nec Aspera Terrente*: 'Let Nothing Deter'.

Looking back I saw a lone figure some distance away. Jack Laundman could not know when or if I was leaving, but had kept a lonely vigil. Once well-built, he was now gaunt and emaciated. Averse to making friends easily we seemed to have an affinity for wide open spaces and clean fresh air. He was married to an Indonesian and had tried to persuade me to return with him to Indonesia where he had spent many years as a tea-planter away from his native land. I longed for the white cliffs of Dover but said I would consider it after that. Now our pipe-dream was gone. Holding my head high I passed through the camp gates and heard them clang behind me, but I was not a free man.

— 15 —

SABURO SAKAI AND THE KAMIKAZI

STRANGELY, my guard did not hustle me. Trying to march, I could only hobble as we tramped leisurely for about three kilometres without speaking. On that dusty road I felt a thousand Nipponese eyes on me. Emotionally and physically exhausted I looked up to the shrine where Colonel Petrie had said he would not bow his head, and wondered if they had decapitated him.

Vaguely aware of a sudden commotion I saw a couple of Japanese in their mid-forties being pushed into the gutter. At that age one is old in Japan and they have to make way for the young.

Tokyo, situated on Tokyo Bay on Honshu Island, is the largest and most densely populated city in the world. The figure of 11,688,000 illustrates the numbers that the Allies were up against, and how insignificant were our small forces at the time of our capture by the yellow devils.

Eventually we reached an unknown rendezvous and I was left to wonder how many hours I had left before my extermination. The truth is stranger than fiction and I relate my experiences as they occurred. I have never gone out of my way to seek the limelight but it has often sought me.

A large six-wheeled troop transporter drew up, followed by a military staff car. A mixed contingency of forces alighted to stretch their legs. Navy, Air Force and Military, they were neither hostile nor violent, merely glancing at me in curiosity, I was of no interest to them. Their stop was just coincidental.

Lighting a cigarette, an Officer walked across and offered it to me. I took it, but no such offer was made to my escort who stood rigidly to attention. After some exchanges they saluted and bowed their heads in the usual Japanese manner, then my guard was dismissed.

Waiting in trepidation, wondering what was to become of me, I had no illusions about the ultimate outcome. The Japanese Major stared at me and I returned the look, hoping he would not strike me for my insolence, the usual punishment in camp. He beckoned to his orderly who brought a bottle and flask-cup from the car, which was filled and handed to me. I tasted it warily, immediately recognizing it as saké. Not much of a drinker, I had not had anything stronger than Pepsi since leaving Egypt. After my long trek from camp, I was thirsty and drained the cup. I remember little else apart from being bundled into the car amid hilarity and raucous laughter from the following vehicles. Perhaps only for the moment I was being treated exceedingly well, but I must have passed out and they let me sleep.

Half-waking, I was seeing the face of Jack Laundman; he would have no-one to converse with now. The exception was Von Boser the Berliner, if Jack would give him half a chance. Von Boser got caught up by accident in the Dutch Colonial Army while visiting the Netherlands East Indies. Every inch a Prussian, he was tall and gaunt with the teutonic air of the vulture. Why I thought of him in my present circumstances I do not know, for I was a condemned man.

I later learned that the servicemen were home on leave to give the Japanese people a morale boost. They were specially selected from front-line service to show the Provinces the might of Nippon, but could not visit their homes. This was the order of Prime Minister Tojo and was inspired by Emperor Hirohito.

When fully awake I realized that I had been transferred to a large truck and had a Nip standing over me. His uniform was grey-green (not the usual dirty yellow of the Army as worn in the jungle) and he did not wear the usual split-toe boots.

His face was unlike the average Japanese, refined with pale unblemished skin that would be the envy of many a woman. He reminded me of a Prince I had met in Saburai, from the Royal House of Bali, an island off the southern tip of Java, just before my capture. He had given me some banknotes depicting his parents and a sister. Both the ladies' breasts were bared. Regrettably the notes were confiscated. His magnificent guitar playing and soft lilting South Sea singing had surprised me.

The convoy reached its destination in a huge complex of extremely ornate buildings. The young Air Force Lieutenant motioned me to follow him. There was no visible guard and it appeared to be my guide's residence. The *tatami* mats and latticed rice-paper doors were the usual, but here resemblance to other dwellings ended. This was indeed the end of the 'Yellow Brick Road' and I awaited the 'Wizard of Oz'. He spoke perfect English but would not explain my presence here until I had bathed in a *ryokan*.

Clean and spacious, one soaps outside the tub, rinses, and then soaks and relaxes in the tub. This was private, not communal. Taken to my sleeping quarters, I was shown a futon laid on the floor. A meal was served to us after my bath. We sat cross-legged on the floor facing each other but I knew very little of Japanese culture. I was aware of the other's scrutiny and asked what we were eating (although I cared little for I was ravenous). Fine features set in a half-smile, he said *'Sukiyaki'*. I was to have this several times before I left. There was no shortage of anything here: thin strips of beef (too tender for water buffalo), accompanied by sliced green onions and many vegetables, but I could only identify *dykan*. There were chunks of soya-bean curd and *shirataki*, a gelatinous noodle simmered in a mixture of rice wine, soy sauce and sugar. All were prepared at a low table. He gave me instructions in the correct use of chopsticks. I had no reason to believe him unfriendly but it crossed my mind I was the lamb for the slaughter. He must have read my thoughts for he said, 'You are safe while you remain in my charge.'

After my meal I thought of the treachery of the Japanese comparable to the Nazis, heinous crimes against women, children and defenceless people. Crimes were committed against whole nations in the Far East and Europe, although to some degree Rommel proved himself to be an Officer and a gentleman.

I addressed my host and asked if he was aware of the felonious treatment meted out in their POW camps? He did not immediately reply, so I told him and he did not interrupt me until my steam was spent. Raising his arms, with a quiet smile he spoke: He was very much aware of the treatment of prisoners. He had heard of the many deaths for which he as a human felt grave sorrow, but felt he must quote the British cliché that 'all is fair in love and war'.

He understood my puzzlement at the present situation but would reveal all in good time. He was not about to practise blood-letting. I can't record his speech exactly but it was deeply ingrained on me, though I did not forget that the Nips are usually most amiable when planning obscenity.

His next words lifted my morale sky high: the war should soon be over in Europe and the Far East and we should pray that there would be no more wars, but he would not live to see the end. Such a bold statement from a youth was beyond my comprehension. His family had been wiped out in the bombing of Tokyo. He was a Samurai, a warrior.

He briefly explained that Samurai were once warriors but now were a small nucleus of elite, following a strict code of behaviour called *bushido* (the way of the warrior). He wore an *obi* or long brown sash which held his swords and costume together. I hoped his swords would remain sheathed.

He talked so long that more food was brought, *sushi* and soya-buckwheat noodles. We drank small amounts of Suntory whisky and beer like fine German lager. The conversation went on into the night and, avid for knowledge, my desire for sleep receded. This was a dream world for me and I suppressed forebodings. Impatience destroys the atmosphere of the East, and his way was of the East.

After a short sleep I awoke at day break to freshly laundered clothes. Green tea and cakes were served and I was ready for a new day. I was taken to the main room where my host stood to greet me with the customary bow; we sat cross-legged facing each other as before and I asked why I was there. He asked for patience while he told me of his past so that I would understand more clearly. He had trained with the RAF, had many British friends and was sad about the war. He talked of RAF Finningley, Church Fenton, Biggin Hill and the Training College at Cranwell. It was uplifting to hear familiar names. He talked of the history of London with obvious enjoyment, knowing more of it than I did. At last he reached the crux of his story. Involved in the raid on Pearl Harbour he regretted how it had been carried out. It was unsavoury as no war had been declared with America up to that point. He would say no more, not wishing to be accused of treason, for his family reputation had to be preserved and for them he must not lose face.

Predominant in Nippon, no one must lose face whatever

crime was committed. He announced with pride that he belonged to the elite corps of Kamikazi. I did not know what he meant and asked him to explain. Kamikazi meant 'wind of God'. The 'Kamikazi Flyers' were a suicide unit of the Japanese Imperial Air Force. 'Flying Bombs' with no undercarriage were to be released from aircraft carriers with the pilot on board. A special launching kite was being built at phenomenal cost. An enterprise costly in human life like this had never been attempted before.

He saw it as a master plan to end the war if they could find enough planes in the time allotted, to sink the fleet of the so-called most powerful nation in the world. It would be a great achievement and would certainly end the conflagration. He asked if I was happy at the thought of my early release. My answer was aggressive when I said that in no way would the Allies be influenced by such an elaborate plan. Our people would have counter plans and it would be better in human terms if the Kamikazi were grounded and he forgot his suicide mission.

He did not take offence but grinned, which I thought was extraordinary. Drawing his sword he sprang to his feet, in Samurai fashion stretching himself up. I did not regret my words. His voice rose an octave and I found his pitched staccato words hard to follow. Abigail, his handmaiden, sat quietly with head bowed and hands neatly folded across her chest, smiling and flickering her eyelids to convey that there was nothing to fear. He paused and lowered his sword, placing it between us with the point towards himself in the position of hara-kiri. He was not to know fear, but however dedicated to the cause of the great Nippon nation he could have no wish to cut his young life short.

After this exhibition he apologised profusely and, bowing out of the room, he returned with a roll of parchment. The Scroll of Honour was a citation – the Japanese equivalent of a summons – signed by Emperor Hirohito and countersigned by the dreaded Premier Tojo. He explained that it was summons to a mission that would be his last. He must hold himself in readiness to end his life but Kamikazi pilots were allowed 'a final honour leave of absence'. They were not refused any request they might make upon the State, and had to be endowed with the best the country could offer.

My host had requested the company of an Englishman, not high ranking but someone he could talk with. I asked if I had been chosen and he said that it had been arranged with Major Tanaka and I was not to worry as the war in Europe was nearly over.

In a sense the Kamikazi were the millionaires of the nation for the brief period of their leave. He was confident that Japan would hold out against all odds just as Great Britain had done in the 'Battle of Britain'. He and his comrades wished to emulate Douglas Bader. When he had been shot down in France, he had been an air ace without legs, which amazed the Germans. (I had run into his squadron in Sumatra.)

He continued to tell me he was commissioned to fly a new Naval suicide attacker, *Ohka* (Cherry Blossom), which was really an anti-shipping missile. The brain child of a Naval airman called Ensign Mitsuo Ohta, they had 150 of these and perhaps another six hundred nearing completion The theory was that the war would soon be finished in the East in favour of the Japanese. The Japanese Air Force was more powerfully equipped and better organized than the Allies surmised, with fighters two-thirds faster than those used in the Battle of Britain. Confident of success, my host was carried away with much detail.

I would be returned to camp in a few days but no one would know what had happened to me during my absence (for my own protection). There was no way he could alter the course of events, I was a prisoner and not a guest of the Japanese Nation. (Tojo's words were repeated parrot fashion.) When I reminded him that my presence was his choice, he reassured me that all would be done to make me comfortable for the next few days in this special place for the Kamikazi. Halfway between Hiroshima and Tokyo, near to Shin Osaka, it was a place for rest and entertainment before their missions.

During this period I felt the lifeblood surge back into my veins and was interested in all I saw and heard. All I had heard of Japan in better days was here, cosy tea-house, tranquil beauty of the garden, serene temple and lovely houses lining the streets. It was unreal and difficult to assimilate.

After three years I had become indoctrinated to prison walls, which afforded a measure of protection; stripped of all superficial civilization one knew exactly where one stood. Friendless and deserted by mankind, none can count on more than three friends when it comes to the crunch.

Although easily exhausted I wanted to see all. Weighing about seven stone fully clothed, this was not to be a convalescence, but I had no intention of yielding my life easily to the heathens. In Kyoto, a major city, I questioned the kind of hostility we would encounter from the inhabitants because of my presence. With pointed sword the message was clear, that not even the Emperor himself would dare to challenge the Kamikazi, especially a Samurai. He proudly adjusted his *obi* and looked for my approving nod. He remarked: 'You are a very agreeable infidel,' and quoted Disraeli: 'My idea of an agreeable person is a person who agrees with me,' and those are my sentiments too!

Ignorant of the geography of Japan, I learned of the best of their way of life, quite an education although I was convinced there was no best side to the Japanese.

A whole day for rest and meditation was now given to me.

Taken to see Sumo, traditional Japanese wrestling at a fifteen-day event organized for the Forces, we watched several bouts. The winner of a tournament was awarded a champion's flag and money. The highest honour was to have his name engraved on a trophy which was the award of Emperor Hirohito. Many high-ranking Nippon were present, also Nazi and what appeared to be Chinese Officers but they may have been Korean. This interested me as Japan in the Second World War wanted the conquest of China. I referred to this later to be told that to the Japanese the Chinese were regarded much as the Free French were to us. Although Communists they had chosen to show allegiance to Japan in the hope that the Chinese nationalists led by Chiang Kai-shek would be driven out. They would then become a world power and play an important part in world affairs along with the victorious Axis powers.

Both proud, neither of us could envisage the defeat of our own country. We watched judo which I found difficult to understand, then visited the Silver Pavilion, the Ginkakuji, originally built in the fifteenth century for the Ashikaga Shogun and converted into a temple on his death. We visited the Kyoto Gosho, 'The Old Imperial Palace', the residence of the Imperial Family until the Meiji restoration in 1868 when they moved to Tokyo.

It was customary to apply for permits from the 'Imperial Household Agency' well in advance to visit the Palace but the royal prerogative was much in evidence and nothing was refused these Kamikazis. For me, a stranger in paradise, there seemed to be no restrictions to my presence in hallowed places.

We met several of the suicide pilots who mystified me by their joviality. They showed no regrets. Brainwashed in the belief of their air supremacy, I hoped they would become quickly disillusioned when they showed me pictures of their invincible aircraft. Only the *Ohka* remains indelible on my mind. They boasted like schoolboys of their exploits knowing there was no way I could pass this knowledge on.

I fervently hoped for a wind of change to stop this world-wide warfire. I had a premonition that it would end with a ball of fire of a kind not previously witnessed. In early childhood I was frequently tormented by a constantly recurring dream, a terrifying vivid nightmare from which I always awakened screaming with fear. I rushed towards the earth at terrific speed from the darkness of outer space towards the round yellow ball of Earth which appeared to be consumed with fire. Not even the comfort of my mother's arms could alleviate the terror.

We climbed to the highest terrace of the Kiyomizu Temple from a height of 160 feet and stood looking down on Kyoto. There was no evidence of bombing here in this beautiful city in the heart of enemy territory. There were numerous shrines. We watched fishermen guide flocks of cormorants by torchlight for the sweet-fleshed *ayu*, a trout-like fish. But this was not a holiday and I had to remind myself that my presence was due to a well-placed Japanese whose last wish was to entertain and talk to an Englishman before he died.

On my final night we visited the Nippon theatre in a huge conference hall. There were no seats and the audience in national dress squatted around in what I thought were family circles on *tatami* mats. They were of the better educated class as evidenced by the elaborate silk kimonos worn by the ladies. There was only low key approval for the actors, no loud clapping. We were watching an ancient form of Japanese court-dance called *Noh* meaning 'Performance'. With only a pine tree painted on the backdrop, the effect of the ornate costumes was enhanced. The audience were obviously connoisseurs despite the small response.

A play followed with actors moving about the stage as did the scenery while the play was in progress. The performance ended on a rostrum in the middle of the hall directly in line with the centre of the stage. A large Nippon flag was lowered from the roof, then what I assumed to be misguided victory speeches began, with much ranting and noise but little response from the audience. Those in my immediate circle looked extremely bored until I was brought abruptly to my feet and a white square with 'Atchi-du-Atchi' written on it was pinned to my chest, before I was led to the centre of the arena to mount the rostrum. Resistance was useless.

Some kind of explanation was being given for my presence. There I stood in front of press cameras, lights flashing, with the Nippon flag behind me; it must have looked as if I was delivering a propaganda speech to the Japanese. This would not look good in anyone's book. I waited with as much dignity as I could muster, then enlightenment dawned as Saburo Sakai stood up and threw his arms wide as if in gesture of entertainment, so I burst forth with a song seeing a vision of the last three years of torture, sacrifice and death. Nothing had changed. Applause rang out and I was delivered from the lions' den.

As I was led from the theatre my young host was awaiting me, his face now sad. 'My time has come, and you must be returned to captivity for a short period. The war in the Pacific may soon be over and our great Nippon nation will assert itself upon the world.' I said nothing, just saluted and bowed. It was goodbye to Saburo Sakai.

With very little ceremony I was bundled into the waiting truck which looked like a British box-car. I wondered how it had been obtained. My three lucky days of liberty had ended swiftly and ignominiously, and now I was bound for an un-known destination, but for a short while I had lived in peace.

Thankful for the privilege of seeing the outside world again, I did not know why it had happened to me. Three days in Kyoto had seemed like three weeks.

I recalled seeing defenceless guinea-pigs endeavouring to hide, in abject fear, from hawks perched at the top of aviary-shaped cages. When the birds swooped the Nips stood viewing the spectacle with hilarity, and I had wanted to vomit and longed for normality. Beyond doubt nations all have hereditary traits which cannot be eradicated.

The departure was rough but I surrendered to sleep. Brought back to reality with a sharp pain behind my right ear, the guard had awakened from his snooze and thought it time for me to wake also. To him I was just 'Atchi-du-Atchi', a prisoner of war.

16

THE INEXPLICABLE EXPERIENCE

R ELUCTANT to return to camp, there was nowhere to run, as my guard tumbled me unceremoniously from the back of the truck. A thickset Korean, my condition was no match for him. Passing through a small village, we had stopped to load logs at a timber yard when some low-flying planes circled overhead. Bombing was concentrated on one target from which great plumes of smoke and flames rose, filling the air with loud explosions. We were in a huge ammunition dump camouflaged as a saw-mill and timber yard. The smoke and cordite from the aircraft choked but there was no retaliation from Japanese aircraft.

All around were shrieks of agony. Tinder homes were aflame and civilians were all mown down by machine-gun fire. As in the desert, and together with my guard who appeared to be the only military personnel, I stayed where I was. I saw the US Air Force markings on the planes which must surely have come from an aircraft-carrier and I felt renewed hope that the Allies must be near the Japanese mainland. When they withdrew to regroup, I crawled into an open sewage drain to avoid injury. I lay as did my guard in the slime, contemplating that no prisoners would survive this kind of onslaught in the last days of war. The pretentious hospitals in the camps bore no Red Cross markings. I pulled a piece of sheet-iron almost across my trench and from the bits of aircraft flung around I could see this place housed more than ammunition.

An aircraft bearing RAF red, white and blue circles flew across my line of vision, taking photographs of the carnage. Holding my head aloft my confidence was shaken when machine-gun bullets sprayed everywhere. I noticed a dead Japanese woman with her baby still strapped to her back. Dressed in dark-blue overalls she had been helping to load timber. The women employed on manual labour worked far harder than the men, who only appeared capable of giving orders. I was reminded of the pretty girls spreading tar on the roads in Ceylon.

The Yankees returned in untold numbers and aggressively resumed their carpet-bombing. With no opposition it seemed to me like kicking a lame duck. With burning earth all around me and a searing pain in my side, in desperation I called the Nip guard who was twenty feet away. He approached with abject fear on his bloated face. There was a blinding flash and the whole area erupted. While I struggled to retain my mental faculties the guard stumbled and fell across me. He grasped a heavy stake no doubt intended for me. As he rolled over I could see his leg had been severed below the left knee.

Somehow I struggled free of the trench and discovered I had been hit by a rock churned up during the height of the raid. I was blood-spattered from the guard and, looking back, realized I could not leave him in his agony. He watched my every move like a hawk and, mistaking my intention, warded me off like a wild-cat as I tried to use some rope which I tore from the tarpaulin sheet on our ill-fated wagon, to tie a tourniquet. A left to his jaw remedied the situation. No longer an enemy, just a pathetic little figure which seemed to have shrunk, a dying man. Gripping his hand, I tightened the tourniquet around the stump of what remained of his leg, then sat exhausted. I thought of Kyoto, then must have lost consciousness.

Kicked awake, still holding the tourniquet, my limbs so numb

I could not release my hold, a Jap stood over me with his bayonet at my throat. I was roughly dragged away amid curses and rifle fire; this death squad were shooting their own injured. Expecting the same treatment, a strange notion that I saw my Father's face enveloped me, and the words, 'If one has your name on it you will get it.' (He had received medals in the First World War and ironically had instructed Japanese sailors in gunnery while serving on the Flag Ship HMS *Raleigh* on her maiden voyage around the world.)

I was dumped without identification papers at a camp named Kure (had there been a direct route, not far from Hiroshima), and left to fend for myself among a host of nationalities: Malays, Chinese, Dutch, Koreans, even some newly interned German sailors. There were both civilians and military, and some British POWs from a propaganda camp near Tokyo: unusually, they had been well fed up to now. Naturally they were all in cliques intent on their own well-being; arrival on my own created suspicion. My condition was viewed as a try-on and in no way was I accepted, which was much worse than any punishment that could have been meted out. Spasmodic air raids resulted in reprisals against the prisoners. No direct hit was scored but there were casualties from flying shrapnel and collapsed buildings all round the site. Against international law, the anti-aircraft batteries were too close to the camp.

Hundreds more prisoners displaced by the bombing now poured into the camp, keeping the guard busy. Treatment was increasingly rough with each contingent's arrival and I feared a sinister plan for mass extermination to cover up maltreatment. In rooms measuring 10 feet by 10 feet, floorboards two feet apart covered by *tatami* mats, it was ten to a room and standing room only. Cat-sized rats were becoming tame. In truth it was a living hell: no respite, no escape from the stench of dead bodies and excreta.

The words of St Matthew 26: 52–53 came to mind:

> Then said Jesus unto him,
> put up again thy sword into his place;
> for all they that take the sword shall
> perish with the sword.
> Thinkest thou that I cannot now pray to my
> Father, and he shall presently give thee more
> than twelve legions of angels.

We had no angels to save us but twelve legions would have come in very useful as continual cremation of corpses took place. Permission was sought to erect a wooden cross in remembrance. Much negotiation and face-slapping resulted in a white cross made with bare hands from limited material being erected near the mock hospital, with a small repository for the ashes of the fallen.

There was a Chinese business man who supplied the camp authorities with many of the simple luxuries that were almost unobtainable, such as eggs and cigarettes. He had tried to pass parts of a cow to us which were part of the town's monthly ration. Caught and brought to the camp, he was flogged before the prisoners. A lonely naked figure, he was staked out. Feeling I had nothing to lose I kept a silent vigil beside him through the bitterly cold night. There was no interference from the guards who were probably prepared to let Atchi-du-Atchi freeze to death. In the morning mist I felt his pulse; he had joined his ancestors without even a whimper. There was no interference as I unfastened him from the shackles which had cut into his flesh, and I called for help from some passing POWs. A few came forward to help me carry the corpse to the far end of the camp where we cremated him. The request to have his ashes returned to his relatives was refused. He had served them well, but when he extended compassion to the prisoners he was rewarded with an agonising execution.

I was praying beside his ashes in my despair when, gloriously and inexplicably, I saw a vision of Jesus. I implored him to release me from all the remorseless machinations for 'I could not love my enemies'. The timbre of the quiet, kindly voice which spoke to me is indescribable. 'And if any man will sue thee to the Law, and take away thy coat, let him have thy cloak also. And whoever shall compel thee to go a mile, go with him twain. Give to him that asketh thee, and from him that would borrow of thee turn not away. Ye hath heard that it hath been said.' These words were from the Gospel of St Matthew.

It was neither imagination nor hallucination as I was taken firmly by the hand. 'Have faith my son. Thou shalt love thy neighbour and hate thine enemies. But I say unto you, Love your enemies, bless them that curse you, do good to them that hate you, and pray for them that despitefully use you and persecute you: That ye may be the children of your Father which is in heaven; for he maketh his sun to rise on the evil and on the good, and sendeth rain on the just and on the unjust.'

The times I had sung 'I know that my redeemer liveth' from Handel's *Messiah*, yet did not appreciate the true meaning until now. Night curfew was on and dusk had fallen before furtively I reached my billet. I wished to make some record of this elevation to my spirit. I slept a sleep I had not known in months.

It seemed as if I had just retired when with kicks to my back I was dragged to my feet. In a stupor I crawled from the billet as dawn was breaking. Pushed and jostled to the guard-room I braced myself. Searched from head to foot, my arms were forced above my head where I was made to clasp my hands. The camp gates were unlocked and I was pushed through them by a rifle-butt.

It was the final straw as I doubled around the perimeter of the camp over rocky lava-like ground with nothing to protect my aching feet. My clogs had been confiscated. Fifty times around and I would be crippled for life. There was no respite, no sustenance and my thoughts were that these bastards were inhuman. If only they would stop this marathon and let me lie down. Striving to clear my mind I had hesitated in my stride and felt devastating pain at the back of my neck as one of the guards struck me with his rifle-butt. This was my punishment for trying to help the Chinaman. All I saw was a sea of faces, not all Japanese.

Jesus had said: 'If the salt hath lost its savour, wherewith shall it be salted? It is thenceforth good for nothing but to be cast out, and to be trodden under foot of men . . .'

I lay on the rough ground, abandoned in my misery. I do not know for how long for I had no concept of time. Maybe in delirium I heard that voice again: 'A city that is set on a hill cannot be hid . . . But I say unto you, love your enemies . . .'

The light was fading and I knew no more. Pushed to the limits of endurance I was released from all further conscious pain.

17

LEVITATION IN HIROSHIMA

AWARE of being dragged over rough ground, choking on my own vomit, my head throbbed and I ached in every limb. As with misted vision I tried to comprehend what was taking place. A frightening image stood over me. Very tall, with high cheek bones and glaring eyes in a fleshless face, I recognized Von Boser the big Prussian. He was struggling to release my bonds and making efforts to restore my circulation. He tended me with care, bringing me rice gruel. There was no revitalizing substance in it but his ministrations began to restore my faith in man. Not much was said in those first few days. Too ill to converse, I was vaguely aware of others in the darkened room. The prostrate figures were silent and unattended. The smell of mortifying flesh was all around.

Under the supervision of the guards, POWs dragged out the dead and dying. Von Boser stood between me and the working party. He spoke two words: 'Christus vergeben,' and the guards appeared not to notice me so I was bypassed.

I summoned strength to question Von Boser on my chances of survival and ask why he was in Kure. After a pause he replied, 'You are not in Kure,' and explained that I had been brought back to Hiroshima camp unconscious on an improvised litter and left with other dying prisoners in the remains of the camp hospital. A direct hit had been scored on the building and he had volunteered to look after the sick, although there were no medical supplies.

Herr. Von. ~Boset.

His halting English took some time to understand. None of the Japanese quarters had been damaged. There was some devastating news. Jack Laundman had been in the hospital with dysentery from which he would not have recovered, but he had been killed in a raid the day before I was returned to the camp. In my present condition I regretted being a day late.

When darkness fell I decided to rid myself of the smell of decaying flesh in this disease-ridden pigsty. Crawling out, oblivious to the risk of discovery, I hoped to locate my billet to see if it had escaped the bombing. Planes broke the silence of the night and as running feet approached I lay motionless until the Nips passed by. They would be making their way to the improvised 'Death Tunnel'. Taking my bearings from the direction in which they sped I headed for the British section of the camp. There had been no air-raid warning and the planes above ignored the anti-aircraft fire outside. Bombs were jettisoned over a wide area away from the camp and, judging from the high spirals of flashing lights, must have hit their targets.

At last my old billet was reached. No one raised an eyebrow at my sudden reappearance. No comment, no questions. The bombing continued as the defence petered out with spasmodic ack-ack. It was evident the Japanese had spread their armed forces throughout Asia and could no longer defend the homeland.

Knowing how ill I was, the Nips still took me down the mine by the scruff of my neck. The methods of persuasion were such that we were glad to be in the bowels of the earth. There were no fit men in camp but the demands of the mining officials were so great that shifts of workers had to be found somehow and, if not found, food supplies were cut off. The intermittent water supply was contaminated with infectious typhoid. Every day it claimed victims and after each day's shift we cremated the dead.

Returning from a night shift, without breakfast or bath, we lined up awaiting the camp Commandant. Some men fell from fatigue. The arrival of the Commandant brought the announcement of Red Cross parcels. Not each, but one between ten. At last this must be the issue arranged by the Swiss doctor to whom Colonel Petrie had handed the list of complaints. The parcels sent in good faith could not be split; the Japanese had taken their share.

The only solution was to mix all ingredients together and make a cake for the ten men, if we were allowed to. The chocolate, gum, mints and toffees, plus all other bits and pieces, were lumped together, mixed into cakes and baked in rice tubs. Strangely, it stayed as cakes and did not melt as anticipated. We assumed by the concession that the Nippon guard wanted a share, which meant a reduction in our ration. We presented the grinning Orientals with six small cakes, laced with spittle and rancid fat, while the Commandant's had other ingredients even more revolting.

Shortly after this incident, I received the worst shock possible. By some miracle, mail arrived. It was now 1945 and I had not received a letter since 1941, just before leaving Cairo. Mine was postmarked 1942 and was from my mother. I was choked after the first few lines. Five deaths: my father in a bomb blast during an air raid on Hull while on Civil Defence work, a favourite aunt and two dear friends, but almost too much to bear, the fifth was the lady nearest to my heart.

Anguished cries intruded on my melancholia. The guards had found a new pastime. Selecting prisoners at random they were extracting remaining teeth for sport. Many had soft palates due to the diet and had lost all sense of taste. With no solids and no means of maintaining dental hygiene their teeth had decayed.

Blind with anger I ran into the mêlée, and was dragged to the guardroom and thrown down at the feet of Yamamoto. Staring down in fury, he motioned to the guard. Rough-handled onto a stool placed in front of the guardroom, I was glad to observe that the bizarre dental activities had temporarily halted. Another guard appeared and passed a kettle of boiling water to Yamamoto. Still numb from my news, I felt incapable of any emotion as I looked up at the large kettle.

There was an awful silence as Yamamoto stood with the

kettle poised and then a timely intervention. The office door crashed open and Osaka Chui appeared. Much taller than the average Japanese, immaculately dressed, he was a daunting figure. We had not been aware he was in camp. Angrily he advanced upon us and, grasping Yamamoto by the neck, threw him to the ground, water spilling over the guards as he fell. My right arm gripped in a vice, I was almost lifted and set down before him on the other side of the desk in his office. Such action was unprecedented; relations between Commandants and Japanese personnel, still less me, cannot fully be appreciated. Commandants held the power of life or death.

A guard brought tea, a mark of great respect, and a serious occasion to Japanese, but this could be the calm before the storm. We watched each other in silence. I accepted a Nip

16. Forcible dentistry: extractions made *ad hoc* to satisfy the whim of the guards.

Woodbine. Then I was handed an English version of the *Nippon Times*, although it contained no real news like the Japanese papers I had pinched which fortunately were never missed. I concluded that Germany and Italy were finished as they were not mentioned, but only glorious deeds of Japanese forces on land and sea and in the air. The main article told of a Naval-rating jumping over the side of his ship and holding that and another ship apart to avoid a collision, as well as many other more unlikely stories. Putting the paper down, I was motioned to keep it. After several welcome cups of tea I was allowed back to my billet where I lay considering events. After this I was treated with some small respect. Further tragedies occurred, more POWs died as victims of the Nips, or of disease because of them. I could smell freedom and that kept me determinedly battling on.

I meant to do something about the tyranny and aggression, but did not know what, as lack of nourishment took its toll. On a moonless night I crept out of the billet keeping an eye on the sleeping guards. Moving stealthily forward towards the wall of the compound, incomprehensibly I was wrapped in a translucent light. An involuntary movement increasing in rapidity trans-ported me off my feet out of the camp to the Japanese Army quarters. There were pans before me with the remains of cooking fat. I found some bottles covered in slimy grease but, undeterred, scooped up the fat, plugging the tops with cotton-waste, which I always carried for possible first-aid, and plugged each bottle neck, binding them together with a strip of my paper-thin jacket. How could I get back into camp? To be caught outside would be certain death. Standing forlorn, I felt myself raised as by some unseen genie and put down firmly within the camp. The guards still slept and, unaware of whether it would make them sick, I gave each man a mouthful of the fat. No one queried the source of the precious oil or why I was creeping about. It was just accepted, the oil was a lifeline to many of the human skeletons struggling to stand. I could not assimilate how it had happened, but realized I had experienced levitation as wearily I crept back to my bunk to sleep.

Once again I found myself in the 'kaka'. For about two weeks it was my turn to pull the *benjo* cart. With no customary face-masks as worn by the Nips, we used long-handled ladles to spread the liquid onto infertile ground. My sympathy was with the beasts of burden. But I was released at the end of the two weeks. We marched to toil with the Nippon female farm-workers. They were tight-lipped, stunted and weather-beaten with muddy faces. Though I tried hard, I could not find one

17. Between the shafts of *benjo* cart, Hiroshima, 1945.
(Corpse disposal in background.)

147

pretty face among them. It was literally a pain in the buttocks and no way a respite from the mine. Bending in agony, we walked forward in rows. It was not 'we plough the fields and scatter the good seed on the land', for the ignorant Nips here did not know a plough. The instrument used was rough-hewn, more substantial than a broom handle and soon contributed to the formation of large blisters.

Spreading out, each to make an individual furrow on endless land, the POWs fell behind the more adept women. The guards left the fallen where they dropped from sheer exhaustion and thirst. The lash met complaints, so we nibbled roots we dug up, concealing them from our tormentors who carried water only for themselves.

The women ahead wore dark blue padded kimono tops with tight padded trousers sporting a flap at the rear of their posteriors, which they let fall when nature called, not stopping their labours. Not a pretty sight for our glazing eyes. The heavy blade at the end of the pole took on huge dimensions. It was impossible to make any indentation on this tract of barren land. Not permitted to look behind, it was an endurance to stay the course, moving ever onwards.

My stint on the *benjo* cart completed, I was returned to camp and back to the mine, where conditions were even worse than before. With drastically reduced numbers it was impossible adequately to supply a single shift. Now permanently assigned to night shifts I was relieved, for the guards were sleepy and the *shokos* conspicuous by their absence from the coal-face. They slept, or found other diversions with the women in the mine, none of whom were on our own pit-face. Demands rose as the war situation deteriorated, and we feared the Nips would blow the entrance to the mine. Averse to being buried alive, I struggled night after night to finish my shift early, and help

18. Tokyo concert party.

others to do so too: not from heroism, for we had no illusions, the writing was on the wall. After a shift of three metres of coal we were all physically drained yet still had to carry out many men in those last days.

The Commandant was changed yet again, and another set of brutal guards drafted in. I saw them as the death squad. We were kept rigidly to attention for hours on our return to camp, rations were withheld and drinking water cut off for the slightest reason. We lived hour to hour for survival and coherent thought fled.

Detailed to lead various working parties I received blows from POWs and from the Nips for any misdemeanour in the party, the leader being considered just as guilty as the culprit. It was basically a language problem, most prisoners having few words of Japanese, and the guards even less English. They would not accept attempts at explanation. On very odd occasions they found it humorous to say 'good morning', receiving uncouth blasphemies in reply.

The only interlude was a few hours occasioned by a visit of the Tokyo POW Concert Party from a propaganda camp when, because of my repeated attempts to produce 'Robin Hood', I was invited to play the role of Maid Marion. At a later date a photograph of this costumed event was given to me as a souvenir.

I could not forget the mad-eyed Johnny who had tried to commit suicide. He had been incarcerated in a cell behind the guard-room ever since, a demented caged animal, and none had interceded on his behalf. Most of the so-called commissioned men did little or nothing for the rank and file. I never knew units or backgrounds but by coincidence saw one of them discharged as a private soldier at Fulford Barracks, York, in 1946. Many had donned uniforms of various kinds in the chaos of the evacuation of Singapore. Rank had been pulled from the outset. However, the Japanese observed one rule only, Officers did not work, as was reflected among their own.

Deciding to walk straight into the guard-room to Johnny's cell with some rice I had saved, it was knocked to the ground and trampled in. The guard went berserk as I was pounced upon. Johnny's face was red and puffed up as if from constant slapping. His lack of recognition showed that I had failed to convey to him that he had not been forgotten.

I now became an occupant of the camp punishment cubicle, reserved for the worst offenders, four feet square and a little less in height. Constructed of corrugated iron walls, it had strips of rough iron about four inches apart across the top to form a grill.

19. The pit. I was twice an occupant at this camp.

Should an attempt be made to reach the arm through, they would be scored with lacerations. Half-sunk into the ground the floor was rough and damp, with buckets of water thrown in to make it thoroughly wet before occupation. There was no way to lie down or stand up, and the guards constantly kicked at the walls to irritate and urinated on the unfortunates below. I sought to save my sanity with thoughts of a practical nature. I was only one of a multitude of men, but now paid dearly for my indiscretion. I had no food or water for four to five days. I longed to stretch cramped limbs, for in my cramped position I would surely be crippled for the rest of my life. A stupor swept over me.

Rudely jolted by a disturbance above me, I looked up. Von Boser stood between two guards. I did not know why he had come to my aid, for in the camps each Nationality kept to itself. Even the Welsh stayed away from the English, but then the English did not fraternize with me either. My rescuer was a very brave man. The guards did not interfere when he summoned the strength to lift me from the dung-hole and carry me back to my billet. Desperately hungry, I would have retched at the sight of food, and was unable to stand. Von Boser pushed a bowl into my shaking hands whispering 'Hund'. To Germans it was a delicacy, and to him a sacrifice of his ration.

By now, the American bombers constantly flew overhead, taking deadly loads elsewhere. Hiroshima was ignored. Going to the mine, I had noticed American Navy bombers dropping an isolated bomb or two, doing little damage, perhaps a dozen or so casualties. Taking our baths in broad daylight it was not unusual to see mines being laid by aircraft in the inland seas. Not a Nip was in sight until we emerged from our bath.

PART FOUR

18

THE ATOMIC BOMB

B EING COMPELLED to take part in the destruction of a city was most bewildering. Those of us still standing with sleep-filled eyes were frog-marched in the early hours into town. Japanese civilians, including children, taking all manner of tools, pulled down their own flimsy homes. Guards urged us to greater effort; the whole of Hiroshima seemed under martial law. The tasty morsels of dried fish and vegetables sparsely hung outside the homes did little to assuage our hunger, but we were not stopped from eating it. Sudden comprehension dawned: we were forming fire breaks; they expected the city would be burned and we were to be piggy in the middle.

There would be no protection from incendiary bombs. The camp huts were timber, dry wood already scorched black in a process used for one- and two-storey buildings. The outer perimeter was of fresh timber, built like a stockade. We were quartered in a large matchbox. Apart from a few buckets of sand no preparation had been made to meet incendiary bombs. I had no desire to be fried. The small number already dropped had done considerable damage. Only the 'war effort' factories stood any chance of survival. It was assumed the American bombers droning overhead were preparing to turn Nippon into a huge bonfire.

The guards were Regulars and hell-bent on unprovoked violence, even on their own folk, especially the weaker ones, too

20. Kita-Kyushu. A typical camp at Tako, Hiroshima Province;
this photograph portrays the structure in relation to the fire-breaks.

old and infirm to destroy their dwellings. I was unfortunate to witness the unbelievable scalping of people for 'looting'; perhaps they were only collecting their own belongings, they had little enough and lived in abject poverty. But worse was to come as a man was grabbed and beheaded with one swipe of the sword, in front of his family, by a guard.

It would not be long before sadism was practised on the POWs. Though back-breaking, the mine was preferable to this. I feigned sickness, but the guards were hard to convince and I received several blows from rifles which they could not fire without ammunition. Pikes were used to similar effect, but my prayers for oblivion once again remained unanswered.

Back at camp I was given three cigarettes for my demolition

work, and swapped them for rice. It was akin to robbing the donor, but he was delighted with the unexpected pleasure and I needed to keep body and soul together. The next night I was back down the mine.

Devastated emotionally, the contents of my letter were in the forefront of my mind. I worked hard through the night and came to the pit-head two hours early. The practice was to hand in lamps to the deputies and gain the disc for release from the mine, but no guards were waiting for us that morning. My shift companion and I wandered towards the water tower against which we rested our weary backs and enjoyed the sunshine. It was close to eight a.m. by the pit-head clock. With eyes half-closed in unaccustomed sunlight I dozed, but was wakened by the sound of aircraft overhead. Looking across unimpeded landscape to Hijiyama Park, two planes flew at high altitude.

My companion was fast asleep, at the outer right-hand bend of the water tower, which would earn him a kick to the groin if a guard found him, but I did not rouse him. He had worked hard and after the shift we had to stumble up hundreds of slippery spiral steps and through heavy air-doors at each section.

The clock now read 8.15 and it was 6 August 1945. As I gazed at the hill of the Park I idly wondered which of the seven finger-like islands they would bomb, Hiroshima being divided by seven channels. The three scraggy horses standing close by presented a sorry sight with drooping heads; it was long past feeding time. My days in the Cavalry were brought to mind and the camaraderie, but that was a long way away. These beasts only had straw and sawdust and while hauling the pit-props were beaten repeatedly by drivers with whips.

A lone guard appeared, a Regular, which was strange for Regulars did not escort us back to camp. Concentrating on the two dots in the sky, he made no attempt to approach us.

21. The atomic bomb, Hiroshima, 6 August, 1945. A copy from a large canvas which I painted and named Eye-Witness. Exhibited, September 1973, in the 'war pensioners' arts competition: I was presented with a certificate and a silver plaque.

Hundreds of planes used Hiroshima as a flight path. He was still scanning the sky when the planes separated over the city boundaries. They must have been reconnaissance, as the first 'All Clear' had sounded as we left the mine. I dozed and was woken by the soldier leaping and cheering '*Banzai*', with the pony drivers imitating him as though in ritual and pointing to the sky. I could not see much to cheer about but then saw that parachutes were dropping, the plane must be in trouble.

In the brilliance of that blue morning sky my eyes watered. Suddenly a series of explosions rent the air and it seemed as if the whole universe was splitting apart, a fissure opening up before me with the rhythm of an express train and click-click-click as of balls on a snooker table. The light was blinding with awesome colours. My senses did not function. I experienced a great electric shock which ran through my body and a terrible fear lodged in my stomach as intense heat jolted through my frame. I looked into a gigantic rainbow, blues, reds, gold and more colours than I knew, dispersing and merging. A huge black mushroom-shaped cloud, red-flecked, eddying and spreading miles above, enclosed me in a giant oven, its smothering heat searing to my soul. It was difficult to breathe; nostrils on fire, my body was ignited like a combustion engine, and I thought that this was the end of the world. Sharp, searing agony was splitting me apart. The roots of my torso twisted as pain tore into me. I became blind and paralysed.

After an eternity the mists cleared a little. Sightless in one eye and only dim sight in the other I looked for my companion. He was a shadowy imprint on the tower wall, the only thing left standing apart from one of two factory chimneys after this holocaust. The landscape was gone, there was no sign of life of any kind. I was in the centre of a gigantic ashtray and man had been retarded a billion years. We were back to the beginning of eternity when earth was a speck in the galaxy. A rifle with a charred 'monkey paw' was all that was left of the Japanese soldier.

Heavy rain, with remorseless and terrible wind, prevented me from rising. Hail shrieked down like big black marbles but I could only lie in the heat and wind, so much hotter than any desert. A vast and bare khaki-coloured wasteland encompassed me.

My miracle is how I still survived. It could not have been the hand of God that committed this crime against humanity. Wondering if the camp and the night-shift had survived, one man came into my mind, Von Boser. Amid such indescribable devastation there can be no enemies. I lay semi-conscious, with no movement around me. I had seen Hiroshima die.

It seemed like a month had passed; darkness, light or time meant nothing, I felt so ill. A contingent of Japanese soldiers arrived in an open lorry, and a Sergeant hauled me up like a sack of potatoes and threw me on top of I did not know what. My clothes were in shreds. After countless time we came to an emergency station and I was carried inside and placed on a *tatami* mat. With distended stomach I was unable to urinate, but did not expect any medical attention.

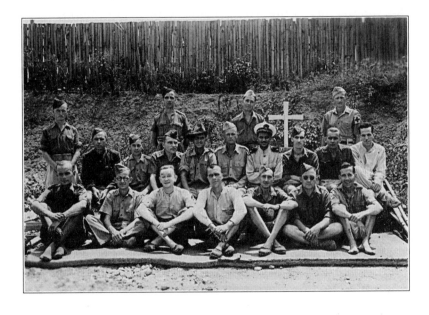

22. Motoyama Hospital assembly point for POWs en route for Wakayama, August 1945. A mixed handful of American, English, Durch and German POWs at a temporary railhead assembly hospital before dispersing. A hapanese photographer took this photograph. When he gave it to me with the loan of a pen most of the men signed it, but I only knew two of them.
Second row: first right, this man had gangrene and did not reach home; *fourth right*: our American Naval doctor who had preserved his uniform for release; *Centre*: in the bush hat – myself, with open wound.

After some time a Japanese in a white coat knelt beside me and laid his equipment on the mat. I had seen these people perform in the Chinese School at Batavia and feared the worst. There was a razor-blade, scissors and thread. I even remember it was black. Without warning I was held down by two Japs as he pressed my stomach. No hygiene, no modern surgical trappings, no sedation, not even chloroform. He incised my lower abdomen with the razor-blade. I prayed and felt no pain. Once he was satisfied he could release no more fluid he sewed me up with the black thread. No attempt was made to stop the bleeding and I passed into semi-coma. I had already noted many others with terrible burns and lost limbs. My neighbour's eyeballs hung from his head. I recall very little else. A doctor shook his head. I doubt if he knew I was a POW but it had gone beyond that stage. Those who brought me in did not differentiate either.

Completely deflated helpers had been drafted in at great risk to themselves. The destruction was so complete it could never be measured in human terms for its excruciating annihilation.

My enforced stay in Kurashiki must have been a month or so and I heard not one word of English in all that time. I was laid in a truck on piles of sacks, and as we crawled along the rubbled streets I could see silhouettes burned into pavements and still-standing walls. Nothing lived, only shadows of the dead. Everything was bleached white. We reached a railhead, and in a huge shed, temporarily named 'Motoyama Hospital', I was pleased to see other prisoners who had come from other parts of Japan. A haggard Japanese officer informed us that we were going to Wakayama, about 250 kilometres from Hiroshima.

The train journey was unforgettable. At two stations where we stopped, no one alighted, but women porters in overalls with clips around their ankles like the field women stood and bowed to the train with great ceremony. Too ill to care about anything beyond myself it was still a relief to see countryside untouched. There was to be no more endurance of cruelty or animosity from Japanese. The mindless behaviour and shabby treatment from now on was to come from our own people.

In Wakayama we were met by a Japanese guard of honour. An Army Captain dropped to his knees and thrust a bunch of flowers into my hands. There was a stunned silence. Between us lay a gulf that could only be spanned by sympathy.

Three and a half years of hell, and now flowers. A Japanese interpreter read a message in halting English which fell more or less on deaf ears. He informed us that we had experienced in Hiroshima the dropping of the first A-bomb, that a second had been dropped on Nagasaki on 9 August, and Japan had surrendered on 14 August. This information did not even produce a muffled cheer. There was only an audible silence.

19

BOUND FOR THE PHILIPPINES

A LMOST TWO MONTHS after the dropping of the bomb, there were still no British personnel to meet us at Wakayama. A solitary Australian Captain tried to pick me out but, intent on seeing my own country, I evaded him.

Hustled down the beaches at nightfall, we stumbled to some speedily erected huts where emaciated POWs were assembling from camps all over Japan. It was an organized rescue mission by American Navy personnel, minus medical staff, but to be leaving Japan was a step back to sanity. Stripped and sluiced down, we were covered in DDT powder from a huge spray. It was suffocating as it penetrated nostrils and went down the throat. Navy jeans and T-shirt were thrown at us but I do not remember any footwear. No head count, no numbers, we were given the first paper plate I had ever seen, onto which was poured some rancid-tasting stew, with insufficient time to eat it before being hustled to landing craft. There was not one word of welcome back to civilization. This omission from the liberators was aggressive to our jaded morale.

Transferred, after a rough ride, to the USS *Sanctuary* (a hospital ship with a multitude of illness on board) there was no sign of even a medical orderly. With an open wound, I had great difficulty, and good luck, in finding the medical store where I cadged a bottle of M&B (May and Bakers) tablets from the storeman. American ships are dry and though the crew queued around the deck for a ration of ice-cream, no offer was made to the British. I was not ungrateful, but cast a jaundiced eye on the abysmal living quarters, cold metal bunks and no heat. There was one blanket per man.

We were set for a rough passage to Okinawa but the crew kept their distance, making no attempt to converse. Entering the waters of the East China Sea we ran into a tropical cyclone, a frequent occurrence in Eastern Asia and very destructive. They are commonly called typhoons and also affect Japan.

The young American sailors had no sea legs and, unlike mariners, slouched about in sloppy fashion, even in calm seas. They were dressed as we were, T-shirt, jean overall-trousers and Naval pork-pie hat. Kept to the steerage end of the ship, never once in our voyage to the Philippines did we see anyone in authority. Our removal from one den only to another had been achieved with none of the fruits of freedom.

In a ship overloaded with American personnel, we were as lepers and suffered more deaths. There were shortages. The ship had proceeded to a catastrophy of great magnitude with not even scant preparation. The Nips at least had tried to give survivors medical treatment, with no drugs or equipment, while still in a stupor from the event. These people did not even administer elementary first aid. That pantomime was reserved for Manila. No attempt was made to swab the decks, the only toil was queueing for their ice-cream. No cigarettes were offered, yet none of us gave any trouble. Apathetic with illness, conversation was non-existent.

Lying on the bunk I shared with two others, I had a visitor. Von Boser had survived. He was a man of few words and no greeting passed between us. He walked straight over to me and said, 'You are Intelligence,' then abruptly walked away. His conjecture baffled me and in my surprise I had not the wit to thank this German to whom I owed so much, and I never had another opportunity.

As the typhoon worsened it was not safe to stay in the bowels of the ship; I felt more secure on the deck tied to the rail with rope. Some of the crew were swept overboard. Crawling into Okinawa Harbour, we saw several overturned ships and more submerged with masts above water. Although anchor chains were dropped our ship made no contact with the shore. With thunderous noise, exploding shells could be heard in the hills; the Nips evidently had not given up. Two days later we weighed anchor and sailed, bound for Manila in the Philippines.

On board, a new type of harassment beset us separately. I was taken to a bare room with dowdy green walls, where a third degree interrogation was conducted by big white-faced men. Their sole interest was in collecting evidence for war files (or so they said), and I was menaced: 'Nothing of this interview must ever be repeated anywhere because our work is highly confidential.' It was an insult to intelligence. We were all further required to supply written details of ill treatment received, and the horrors endured. Excuses were not accepted even from men with cramped hands. Names would be got come hell or high water. Co-operation might have been achieved if there had been at least some Service personnel among them. Rude comments were scrawled on their official papers and I signed myself 'Popeye' as usual.

By now we were heartily sick of Americans unable to relate in any way to the recent existence we had vacated. And in our freedom transit we suffered more needless deaths due solely to medical neglect. I was my own medical staff, crushing my M&B tablets, but I had no dressings. The 'million dollar' friends were as ruthless with us as with their enemies.

Sea sickness prevented our complement from accepting food

almost until we reached Corregidor on the opposite side of Manila in the Philippines. Our arrival and disembarkation down the gangplank was reminiscent of our arrival in Nippon, but minus the bleak Manchurian winds. An American Sergeant yelled from the top of the gangplank, 'Is that the last of the bastards?' Just as in Japan there was no count taken, and when I approached an American Officer to ask for stretcher-bearers for the dying, was told they had nothing for us and no wagons. Full-faced Japanese prisoners were sweeping the docks, dressed in superfine denims and smoking cigars. The time for us crawled, especially as we were not fed, not even a cup of tea.

Eventually we were loaded onto old, open Army vehicles and slowly driven along the promenade. The disgusting promiscuous behaviour of the American personnel with the local girls was on open view all the way. Clear of the promenade, we were driven quickly across rough terrain to a camp outside Manila, about fifteen to twenty miles away. At a speed of sixty to seventy miles an hour the driver suddenly braked and jettisoned his human cargo out of the open truck. Fortunately for me I landed on top of others. Some were badly injured while the rest of us were cut and bruised. We were finally 'dumped' at some marquees being prepared for our occupation.

With still no directive for the POWs it was very much a case of fending for ourselves. Our only concession was a crate of American beer each, but our stomachs were in no condition to drink it. From then on the Americans hung around, interested in our 'issue'. Some sold their beer; I bartered mine for a US Naval uniform. Finally we were fed, along with disparaging remarks about our origins. I longed to see British Service personnel though none arrived, nor did any American do anything to help of his own volition. Despite such treatment the

The journey's end was far from sight as I tried to put the giant jigsaw of life into perspective. My wound was beginning to heal thanks to my self-medication of crushed M&B tablets. Some of the Americans had a rough passage at this stage. Living on the stairways and in the latrines we tripped over them to and from the bog. Seemingly oblivious to their surroundings they played endless games of Crown and Anchor, while the boat rolled, trying to execute a somersault.

In total darkness with no navigation lights we arrived at The Sandwich, better known as Hawaiian, Islands discovered by Captain James Cook. We dropped anchor and watched the flickering lights and activity on the shoreline. The crew became disorderly as liberty boats were expected to take them ashore. In the confusion three of us contrived to join the mob and escaped from the ship unnoticed. We primarily sought some medical assistance for the British contingent but failed abysmally.

Our pleas fell on deaf ears in Honolulu, Hawaii, amid scenes of the utmost debauchery. Sick at heart we found the wharf, but there was no liberty boat from the USS *Marine Shark* so we had to sit tight and hope for a lift back. We had longed for civilization *but this was not it.*

After an incalculable time the same boat which had taken us out drew up to the quay and we promptly got on board, only to be turned off to await the return of the ship's crew. We had not been fed for twenty-four hours but that was the least of our worries. When some of the bedraggled crew arrived we got on board with them, but the boat was not going to move until the whole crew returned. All in all, the wait was for two days and still crew were missing including a necessary piece of equipment: the *engine room staff.* Enlisted men, they had deserted the ship. The dismal harbour was overshadowed with burnt-out hulks of Naval vessels sunk by the Japs while moored at their berths in the harbour. With dismay, hope faded as the crew could not be traced. The Military Police on shore could not keep the peace between warring factions of the Services, let alone find the missing crewmen.

Back on board the *Marine Shark* ex-prisoners from HMS *Repulse* and HMS *Prince of Wales* (both sunk off Singapore in 1942), though depleted in health, checked supplies and the feasibility of taking over. I cannot put words to my admiration of their courage as, without sailing papers or any other documentation, they decided to sail the ship over two thousand miles to San Francisco, with no escort. Once at sea their resourcefulness filled me with pride. After prison privations over three years their courage could not be excelled.

Unlike the riveted British vessels, this 'utility-built' ship was welded together. Though not built to last they were nevertheless vital to our Merchant Navy during the crucial days of war for conveying supplies to Britain. Not old, she had seen better days, and hundreds of miles out of Hawaii she sprung a number of leaks and listed, taking on more water. Eventually, at a list of 45°, I was reminded of the *Titanic*, but this was not the Arctic and at least there were no icebergs to contend with. The water would be warm in the Pacific but the sharks in those waters were the meanest, most bloodthirsty creatures under the sea. They had greedily devoured our compatriots after burial off the *Singapore Maru*, and this could now be our fate. Crowded as we were at this 'list', any moderate breaker would have completed the turn over. I knew in calm seas we could make it, but we were dependent on prevailing winds and currents for a distance of two thousand miles. But our bright lads found the right shipping lanes and the seas remained calm. Against such heavy odds I felt that someone above must have had a sustaining hand in piloting this heap of old junk over such a tremendous distance.

'When I needed a haven dear LORD You were there.'

PART FIVE

20

SAN FRANCISCO, TACOMA, AND

OVER THE ROCKIES

W E REACHED San Francisco Bay with sirens shrieking, and were met by another ship whose name my eyes were too misted to see. On the upper deck a Ladies' Military Band played 'Sentimental Journey Home'; this they did for all returning ships. No tugs came to our aid, we just crawled in behind the ship with the lady soldiers. We dropped anchor under the Golden Gate Bridge, and painted in huge white letters on the Alcatraz prison walls was the word WELCOME.

Eventually we manoeuvred to the dock-side where a crowd of civilians stood. In due course we were mustered on deck by the MPs who had scaled up rope ladders, segregating the Yanks from the British. Our gallant engine men were unceremoniously ordered from their post. Covered in oil and grease, they were not a pretty sight, but to me it was *they* who were the real heroes.

On shore 'bank clerks' appeared with small heavy-laden sacks and emptied dollar bills onto rows of trestle tables. Over the loud-hailer it was announced that all would come separately down the gangplank to receive an individual welcome home and the sum of $3,000, and all rankers would be promoted on the spot to Sergeant. We felt that at last someone cared and the words of the Statue of Liberty were true.

As we groped our way down the gangplank we each received a handclap, with the British being the last to touch the ground and I landed on all-fours as my sea-legs gave way. No helping hand was extended to the obviously sick amongst us and no ambulances or medics were visible. Winston Churchill had promised us 'Blood, Sweat and Tears' of which we had had our fair share; money was our last interest but would at least afford us a degree of independence. Slowly we took up our places in line, where each British man solemnly received the magnificent sum of $8 with which to cross America, then marched at the end of a column through a huge rainbow-shaped archway which had been erected 'Hollywood' fashion with the words 'THRO' THESE PORTALS ARE PASSING THE BRAVEST MEN IN HISTORY'. We had received our individual reception but not once in all the lengthy proceedings were we offered food or drink.

Mustering our pride and soldierly bearing we went forward to the perimeter of the docks. Without warning we were suddenly separated from the main body of Americans by a party of rifle-clicking Marines. Under armed guard once again, realization dawned. While guests of Uncle Sam we were to be treated like lepers. Perhaps they feared contamination of their civilian population. We were moved towards the Oakland Bridge and Angel Island into a huge prison-like enclosure; no direction, no supervision but at least we managed to get some refreshment.

Thrown some ill-fitting Canadian battle-dress with brown boots and tam-o'shanters, we swopped them about to get a near fit. After a night's sleep I decided I was leaving and, securing the interest of two others, despite perimeter lights we escaped through the barbed wire the following night.

Devoid of stamina, sheer will-power sustained us as we hitch-hiked on our way. No longer under any command, British or American, we determined no camp would hold us again. We had no need to thumb, for lifts were offered. At each stopover we earned a few cents by sweeping up, or manning gasolene pumps and washing windscreens, much to the amusement of the Yanks who thought our baggy khaki was a publicity stunt.

We slept rough; it was easy to get lifts on trucks. We also rode in several private cars, once in a shrewish Marshal's, who with sirens blaring invited us to spend the night as 'guests'. We declined, anxious to be on our way, to God knew where. It was not difficult to keep clean and additionally, find abundant eating places, where for a few cents we ate beefburgers and sandwiches thicker than the average mouth could cope with. It was living beyond our wildest dreams but as our stomachs were not as yet up to a lot of food, we exercised discretion.

With no plan in mind we stopped at a farm and helped with the sweetcorn and water-melon harvest. The song was right: the corn *is* as high as an elephant's eye, and it *does* keep reaching right up to the sky. Our feet were in a bad way as the first class Canadian boots were ill-fitting. Life was a novelty in the land of milk and honey and it had not occurred to us how to rejoin the lads in time to return home.

By now 675 miles from San Francisco, we were passing through the outskirts of Tacoma near to Seattle, and at dusk made our way down the main street passing a building under repair. We went to look but, seeing a large amount of jewellery displayed, turned away sharply. We had no wish to be done for loitering with intent.

A floodlight almost blinded us and a gun was pressed to my back; with hands in the air the pause seemed endless. Then with a roar of laughter the security guard invited us into the emporium. We thought the joke in bad taste. He passed his gun to me. Familiar with Smith and Wesson I expressed interest, but thought it was a bit trusting, especially as my companions suggested with a wink to return the joke. With the gun still in my hand we sat down to take the weight off our feet.

Vaguely aware of police sirens wailing in the vicinity we were suddenly spreadeagled against the shop wall by three burly cops. With no identity papers (an offence in itself) how could we explain our temporary absence without leave? I foresaw a long stay in the copshop. My arm was almost wrenched off as the gun was taken from me, then, flung back against the shop wall, I was handcuffed and searched. With a smirk the guard stood to one side just out of hearing and spoke to the police who quickly released us and left as they came.

Our mentor apologised for it and explained that seeing the uniforms he had thought we were Canadian but hearing the accent knew we were British. Stepping into the precinct we had triggered an alarm just set by the police. The premises had recently been held up by gangsters and he pointed to chalk marks on the floor where his predecessor had been shot dead. His mother was English and, inviting us to stay for the night, said he would take us home in the morning to meet her. We needed no persuading after our fright, especially with a hot drink before us.

Mrs Armstrong adopted us into her beautiful home with its spacious garden with lush green lawns. She cooked us roast beef and Yorkshire puddings, and there was a plentiful supply of popcorn and many different flavours of ice-cream. Respect and liking were mutual. There was a pleasant daughter engaged to an Anglican clergyman. Mr Armstrong worked for the FBI in Seattle so we saw little of him, but on a short tour around Tacoma – a civilized Indian village – he took us to see Indian totem poles which had been a frontage to the wigwams of their forebears, beautifully carved and painted.

We visited the American Legion hall decked with a variety of historical flags. It was similar to the British Legion, but members were dressed more elaborately in dark blue serge uniforms with gold trimmings and glengarry hats. We stood before them to be introduced, and were questioned as to where, when and why we had allowed ourselves to be captured. We told them we were overwhelmed by Manchurians, and they asked in one voice: 'Who the hell are the Manchurians?'

Enlightenment was futile in the face of such naïveté. My hand was almost crushed by one legionnaire who gripped it tightly and would not let go.

Anxious to go home, we asked our host how to get in touch with the Military authorities. The Armstrongs were my first real friendship outside prison for three and a half years and lingered on by letter for many years after my return home.

Mr Armstrong took me to the Military HQ in Seattle; I was not impressed by the Infantrymen on rifle-drill with fags in their mouths but made no comment. At this time there was a noisy, vulgar publicity stunt to promote a Betty Grable film. The stars were treated like cattle and told they were only pieces of meat. Accompanied by Mr Armstrong and Bill I was introduced to Betty Grable in her dressing room at the Hotel Seattle. A complete contradiction to her screen portrayals, she was quiet and gracious. Always a favourite of mine it was a great thrill to meet her in the flesh, but she did not show us the famous legs. With the great influence of Mr Armstrong attitudes towards us changed. We had not seen Los Angeles, which was to the south in California. We had turned north, but as things turned out had seen the best of the film city by meeting Betty Grable.

Our fortune continued when our host told us he had been in touch with well informed circles about the movements of POWs. A Canadian Pacific railroad train was due at Tacoma station with a load of Commonwealth ex-prisoners on board and he had made reservations for us on the best part of the train with sleepers and a lounge. We would go across the Rocky Mountains though it was not the best time of year to do so.

After emotional goodbyes we were driven to the railhead (it was not a station in the best English tradition for it had no platform). Mr Armstrong told me our journey *was at the request of the Canadian government* who wanted the British contingent to visit Canada, but it had to be at speed for the *Queen Mary* sailing from New York had been postponed to take us home. We had four days to reach Detroit, passing the great lakes of Superior, Michigan, Huron, Erie and Ontario.

Since 'escaping' from the camp at Angel Island every moment had been spent acquiring knowledge. Two months since leaving the abhorrence of Japan we still carried the indelible scars and nightmares (from which there was no escape). We were impatient with nostalgia to go home. Our train accommodation was as we were told with several seats each, first class conditions with beds above the seats which the attendant let down at seven each night. Meals were also brought to us. There were luxurious toilets and a separate lounge. These were normal Canadian Pacific Railroad conditions considered necessary for a journey of four or five days.

Across the Rockies the temperature was well below zero and a pack of cards on the ledge beside me was frozen solid yet I did not feel the cold. The sheer drops down the ravines and the scenery around were breathtaking. Several engines were used to push our train up the steep inclines and I mused on the miracle men who had laid the tracks in such rough terrain, mountains so steep, where the wilderness looked ominously terrifying in all its snow-capped beauty.

Under my tunic I hid my 'crock of gold'. It may be questioned why I treasured it so much. During my stay in Tacoma I sought something which would be needed and very precious to return with to England. In my pocket I still had the insignificant $8. Looking at the pricey stores I thought my task was hopeless until I reached the last emporium.

On entering the store I nervously approached the lady who appeared to be the manageress and she took me around all the departments. Everything cost well in excess of my meagre fortune. A very pretty blonde in the lingerie department understood my embarrassing predicament and as she had a serviceman brother herself, soon put me at my ease. Her brother had been wounded on the beaches of Normandy and sent to England to recuperate. There he had learned that the most precious currency in Britain was nylon stockings.

My fortune would buy four pairs of nylons and make me more wealthy than I could imagine. Her invitation to share her lunch and have a demonstration of the nylons resulted in my coming away with only three pairs of stockings. Returning to the Armstrongs' with my precious currency they remained beneath my tunic with a treasured memory.

A snow plough preceded the train through many gorges and long tunnels, and most of the time I slept, awoken only by the jerking as the coaches periodically shunted together. The attendant was ever smiling.

Our first stop in a tiny place called Moose Jaw saw local girls bearing blackboards with messages of love, to which – to their disappointment – we did not respond. The Royal Canadian Mounties got on board and showered us with bananas and other fruit as well as countless 'Capstan' cigarettes. I recall the packet with the sailor and lifebelt on them as if it were yesterday. It was our first sight of something British, though the 'fags' themselves were akin to the Italian cigarettes taken from a captured lorry outside Tobruk.

Leaving the train we were shown what I believe was the

Thomson river, teeming with salmon. The sparsely populated town consisted of wooden huts and a well-stocked shop built of galvanised iron sheets. As we chatted with the Mounties I felt the effects of the high altitude.

I much admired the clothing of the police, sable hats with long sable tails hanging down their coat collars, and red tunics visible beneath fur coats. A Mountie told us that they had to be self-supporting throughout long periods of the year except for small luxuries obtained in the spring in exchange for furs. For meat they hunted the seven-foot-high moose. Carcasses were dressed and hung in log cabins throughout the district and anyone could hack a joint off whenever it was needed. Any left over at the end of the winter were left to hang, even in the hottest weather, until maggot infested, when they became quite a flavoured delicacy.

Lighting one of the precious Capstans, the cigarette froze to my lips. Removing it, my lips bled and I was glad to scramble back into the warmth of the train, and away from the men-hungry girls who were not after our money.

Not over-dressed for the climate the girls were pretty but probably outnumbered the men by about ten to one. It was hard to view them as being of the same stock as the unkempt backwoodsmen. We were told that the passes would soon be closed as no snow plough could clear them, so we had to push on if we wanted to get home in 1945. Thanking them for the hospitality we left at break-neck speed to catch the *Queen Mary*.

There were few other stops apart from taking on water and fuel, and these were mainly at night. However, there was one incident of interest. Two railroads competing about a mile apart tried to beat each other on single tracks at top speed, the opposing railway being 'The National'. There were herds of cattle, known to the Americans as long-horned steers, grazing on

POWs' behaviour was impeccable, and it was sad that inevitably some would have to be left in Philippino soil.

We heard that Danny Kaye (whom no one knew) was to give a show. Seeking someone in authority for permission to attend, a Platoon Commander gave us a resounding 'No'. Few were fit to make any journey, but some of us were determined to see some life if it was our last act. At nightfall we broke through the cordon and hitched a lift. Once our identity was known we were ordered off the vehicle but were close enough to the cheering to find our way.

Several thousand troops were seated on the ground in a semi-circular floodlit arena. With a large orchestra pit and a huge stage lit in many colours, I had never seen anything like it for troops, and squatting on the perimeter we had a tremendous view in miniature. Although uproariously welcomed, I thought Danny Kaye's show abysmal, apart from some little girls who had reputedly been prisoners. Prettily dressed, they sang and danced, and I was sceptical that they would perform like circus dogs after being incarcerated in a prison camp.

It was past midnight when we left to miss the stampede and on reaching the centre of Manila we found it was open war between the huge Military Police and any servicemen they could lay their clubs on. Clubbed drunks lay all around. I had seen rough treatment meted out by Red Caps on Italian prisoners at Abbassia, Cairo, but this was wholesale brutality in abuse of authority. With no signposts or tracks to guide us we somehow managed to get back to the camp with the view that Americans were 'all wind and hiss'.

The next day twenty white-coated 'doctors' sat in booths like battery hens to view our stripped bodies. The examination was farcical as they only looked but never deigned to touch. I found only one human being at the end of the line, who exclaimed aloud at my open wound. In a voice charged with emotion a senior medical man told us that a report would be submitted on our condition, and apologised for being unable to do anything for us. 'I and my staff are not empowered to give you any treatment; we have been ordered to look after our own.' A mockery of the tablet at the foot of the Statue of Liberty.

The New Colossus

Not like the Brazen Giant of Greek Fame,
With conquering limbs astride from Land to Land;
Here at our sea-washed, Sunset Gates shall stand
A mighty Woman with a torch, whose flame
is the imprisoned lightning, and her name
'Mother of exiles'! From her beacon-hand
glows world-wide welcome; Her mild Eyes command
the air-bridged harbour that twin cities frame.
'KEEP ANCIENT LANDS, YOUR STORIED POMP' cries she
with silent lips, 'GIVE ME YOUR TIRED,
your huddled masses yearning to breathe free,
The wretched refuse of your Teeming Shore
Send these, the Homeless tempest-tossed to me,
'I lift my lamp beside the Golden door!'

Emma Lazarus 1930.

A diversion occurred in the big Mess marquee where we were unexpectedly addressed by Lady Edwina Mountbatten. Dressed in a skirt and blouse and wearing a head scarf and no make up, she looked like any ordinary British housewife, an uplifting sight to our disillusioned eyes. Unaccompanied by either British or American officers she stood on a mess trestle table to have a good view of us all: 'I regret I have no authority here, all I can say is get as much lovely American food down you as possible, for you will not get it when you are returned to Blighty.'

Her English voice was music to our ears. She was shocked by what she saw. She concluded with, 'My man is fighting for you in Burma.' She felt her inability to intervene on our behalf just as much as we did. Making a quick departure to her vehicle we did not seek to detain her. We had no wish to add to her distress.

We embarked on *Marine Shark*, a cargo vessel, which was already packed with humanity, American prisoners of war and women ex-prisoners from China and elsewhere. The women had dehydrated skin, terribly wrinkled and yellow, as they lay about the deck. Our destination was the Hawaiian Islands, over five thousand miles ahead. The Tannoy announced that we were to be privileged with an English cup of tea. Inevitably it was served cold with no milk or sugar, but we were glad to receive anything.

Two days later another treat was in store for us. A cinema show was to be given on the upper deck, for 'BRITISH ONLY'. We could not understand the discrimination but no man refused this unexpected pleasure. It was the best evening for a long time. There was a gorgeous twilight with a calm sea. Approaching the upper deck I noticed neatly unrolled fire hoses on either side and presumed them to be fire precautions.

Installed in orderly rows before a sizeable screen and anticipating the 1935 film of Bette Davis and Franchot Tone in 'Dangerous', we were oblivous to the bustle around from the crew 'going about their duties', until without warning, 'whoooosh' – they had turned powerful hoses on us, and from the Captain down to the lowest deck-hand, they screamed with

23. 'The Shark's Teeth'.

raucous laughter. All were in on the so-called joke except of course the victims. An extremely sick body of men, our frail forms did not appreciate their warped sense of humour. This was only one of more numerous incidents using the British as the butt of their childish jokes.

Meanwhile we lost more of our men who were buried at sea without the Union Jack or even a Padre's blessing to send them on their way. Issued with a copy of the New Testament printed in American slang I opened mine and read: 'The Lord said Okay . . .' Disgusted, I promptly slung it over the side, but how I later wished I had kept it as a souvenir.

the plains with icicles up to a foot long dangling from their jaws. This was followed by wooded land with tightly packed saplings growing in unbelievably vast forests. We passed two husky woodsmen felling trees and the attendant told us anyone could have as much land as they could clear in three years. After three years they registered their claim with the Canadian Government and became the legitimate owners of the land, free of charge.

Fort William on the shores of Lake Superior was our last stop. Arriving close to midnight we were greeted at a floodlit railhead by a fully kilted Scottish-Canadian Ladies' Pipe band. All wore bearskins. There were no civilians or Forces personnel other than the semi-military band, a body of much appreciated fine healthy lasses. Regretfully we had only one hour there and two ladies, more Scottish than the Scottish, promised to write, which they did for two years after my return to England. It was still freezing cold but I envied their tartan kilts and easygoing lifestyle.

At last in Detroit we said goodbye to the railway crew as the attendants lined up in smart spotless white tunics, blue serge trousers and tippie hats. They had been good friends during our four-day journey and, unable to tip in cash, we passed over the cigarettes lavished on us by the Mounties, which they genially accepted.

21

JOURNEY HOME

O<small>N</small> a small American steamboat which had no surrounding rail we left Fort William with five hundred miles ahead of us and ran into a blanket of fog. Neither cover nor cabins were available, but I slept, remembering little of the journey until the Eastern States of America loomed out of the gloom as we reached the Hudson.

Our river boat seemed to make little progress and, although warmer, the ship's sirens muffled by fog sent shivers down my spine. The crew moved around in silence, slopping back into the gloom as we abruptly stopped, docking at Long Island in the USA. We lost our bearings in the ensuing mêlée and two of us asked a member of the crew where the gangplank was. He pointed to the port side of the ship and in thick fog with no safety rail my companion was the victim of a deliberate mistake as he disappeared over the side. I heard the splash as he hit the water and knew he was swimming for his life below me.

Fortunately there was a boat-hook at hand and with it I was able to grope about the water in the direction of the distressed cry. On the second attempt there was a pull on the pole, and now figures came out of the gloom to help me. Not the crew members but our own men. Somehow he held on in the swift flowing current of the Hudson and, gathering strength, we hauled him on board. On deck we pumped the muck out of him till he could breathe more normally. He was covered in black slimy oil, which could have been my own fate but for the grace of God, for there was only one boat hook.

We made our way in silence to the quay for a long wait before the Customs officials arrived to take us to a more civilized part of the docks. There were powerful gantry overhead lights trained upon us, but no one knew what to do with us. Cold, damp, miserable and in desperate need of blankets, the loud hailer announced that all would be provided for us on the *Queen Mary*. Aided by the lights of New York we could just make out a huge hulk through the fog in the middle of the river.

Fearing hypothermia for our comrade who lay oil-soaked and showing little sign of life, I appealed to a police officer for a stretcher and blanket. I received the usual blank stare before he turned away. Glad to leave such inhospitable shores we were loaded once more onto river steamers and after another four hours on the dockside we reached our mother ship.

Much later in London I met a British Major who had returned from America, and who was supposed to have met us and liaise on our behalf. When asked, 'Where the hell were you on that cold desperate night?' he grinningly confessed he was having a 'swell time'. Obviously one of the 'I'm all right Jack' brigade.

On board the *Queen Mary* it was totally disorganized. There was no one to receive or direct us and no sign of the ship's crew and officers. Orders boomed through the loud speakers: All our cabins would be in the steerage end of the ship, to which we must find our own way and sort accommodation out between ourselves. On this foggy night, long past hunger pangs, the search eventually brought us to the beautifully wood-panelled main stairway, opening onto vestibules and antechambers with shops no longer occupied. We also found the below-decks swimming pool, boarded over.

The ship was divided into different colours and each deck bore a different letter of the alphabet. I was on 'D'.deck and my colour was blue. Great watertight doors effectively cut us off from the forward part of the ship and everywhere the panelled hallways had been stripped of carpets.

With several strangers I entered the cabin. Walls and iron bunks were dull, lifeless khaki. Two Army blankets were tossed on each bunk, and there were no pillows. Being above the engine room for several days of this did not hold much promise of sleep. How could they be such ignoramuses about our vital medical needs? Then came the ultimate inhumanity when the Captain announced, 'Unless you people report for kitchen police duties' (peeling spuds, washing dishes etc.) 'the ship will not sail.' Lumped *en masse*, all ranks, sick, lame, hungry, tired and sorely tried we were not even offered a hot drink so, advising my companions to sit tight, I severed the speakers to avoid any further harassing announcements.

Finding the odour of my clothing offensive I went up to the sun deck. It was enclosed for the winter months but not deserted. My startled gaze fell on a throng of men and two British Auxiliary women, who, oblivious to their professional duties, were practising with no shame, but it was not medicine. Turning my back I went to the stern of the ship and sought the kitchens to get food for myself and my companions still in the cabin. Returning by the sun deck the two women were now minus skirts and stockings with men grabbing at them from all sides as they danced a couple of steps with each man to some canned music. It must have been a tough journey for them as they were not sighted again after the first night. Was this the 'Brave New World' for which we had borne so much? I grieved as I remembered the letter bearing the news of the death of my father and among others the lady closer than most, who died because of such irresponsible behaviour while I was thousands of miles away. In the depths of my bitter grief, turbulence of anger grew.

'I am'

I AM! yet what I am who cares or knows?
My friends forsake me like a memory Lost.
I am the self-consumer of my woes;
They rise and vanish, an oblivious Host.
Shadows of life, whose very soul is Lost,
And yet I am – I live – though I am Tossed
Into the nothingness of scorn and Noise,
Into the living sea of waking dreams
Where there is neither sense of life, nor joys
But the huge shipwreck of my own Esteem
And all that's dear. Even those I Loved the best
Are strange – nay, they are stranger than the rest.
I long for scenes where woman never smiled or wept,
There to abide with my Creator, God,
And sleep as I in childhood sweetly slept
Full of high thoughts, unborn. So let me lie.
The grass below; above – the vaulted sky.

With such anguish in my soul I returned to the deck, passing the now languished foray, to the stern. Desertion by my own people had achieved something the Japanese had failed to do during the whole of my captivity: my unflagging spirit was crushed and bleeding. I was a stranger to myself.

As I stood on the stern of the deck, inexplicably I became enveloped in the lights of many colours, similar to those exuded by the atomic bomb of Hiroshima. It could not be the Aurora Borealis, for this was a ship in the middle of the Atlantic. How

I reached my cabin I do not know but awoke in my bunk stiff and aching from head to foot. The unheralded experience had confounded my emotional exhaustion into a dreamless sleep.

Much of my life had been a ghastly nightmare but the ship was real enough when I dragged myself to the now deserted deck. I climbed over the dividing rails between the storm-tossed steerage and the forbidden territory beyond, passing the lifeboats swaying on their davits. I wanted to put as much distance as possible between myself and the rest of humanity. Such a desire was impractical within the confines of a ship yet I met no one in my explorations.

The howling gale almost claimed me as I clung to the rails to reach the superstructure beneath the bridge. There was still no sign of life. Aghast by the violence of the gale which was most frightening in its power I was pinned down. I could not move to achieve the challenge to myself (of getting to the port side by going beneath the bridge).

The Captain was endeavouring to break the record by crossing from New York to Southampton in four days. He wanted the much desired Blue Riband, a great achievement for an ocean liner. Regrettably the turbulence of his passage deprived him of the target by just a few hours.

Prior to disembarkation, Custom officials fruitlessly turned over our cabins. There were no farewells from the ship's crew and not a soul to greet us. We were just a few hundred exhausted men. Completely burnt out we were an embarrassment to our native land, which still failed to produce the elusive medicine so urgently needed.

War in Europe had only been over for a few months, but not long enough surely to forget the men and the incidents in *all* theatres of war. Shown to some Nissen huts close to the docks we were instructed to stay put, which was a pointless instruction as we did not have a cent between us. We acquired new Army battledress and underclothes. On my one foray into the town I met no one of interest to me; the sentiments of the locals were mutual. Ladies of easy virtue haunted us and put the fear of God into me. Having come this far without mishap it was going to stay that way and they did not get my nylon currency.

A convoy of trucks arrived to take us to the railway station, and I gladly gathered my kit, eager to be on the final lap home. Conditioned to servicemen routed through their town, I doubt if the residents of Southampton were aware of our presence.

The first batch of POWs from the Far East, our homecoming was ignored by the State. Much later Lady Astor announced in the House of Commons that 'All POWs from the Far East should wear yellow arm bands.' Outcasts from the start, official attitudes have not changed.

The ladies of the night followed us onto the train for Waterloo, actively encouraged by the railway police. They had no tickets and this was harassment that could well be done without. The train was transformed into passion coaches as men were pursued from compartment to compartment. Marlene Dietrich in *The Blue Angel* had nothing on them. They revelled in their licence, baring all throughout the journey. This was the end product of the war to end all wars. I was unaware of the birth of a new promiscuous era in my absence and found such degrading scenes deeply offensive.

There was a tedious wait at Waterloo devoid of cups of tea, before Army vehicles came to take us to departure stations for our home towns. My destination was Kings Cross for Hull and Yorkshire.

A Captain Campbell, in full Scots uniform with kilt and sporran, was in charge to escort us across London. With a handful of official papers he had made straight for me with no handclasp of friendship or the greeting for which I craved; he uttered one word, 'Bandung'.

In the heat of the Japanese advance in the mountainous country surrounding Semarang on our way to Tjilatjap on the southern coast from which we had hoped to escape, there had been two gallant officers who had stolen the staff car and weapons from myself and Duke, the Indian. I had met Captain Campbell in General Headquarters in Java and he now challenged me to agree to a court-martial of the Captain (one of the offenders). He did not tender the source of his information and nor did I ask. I was just too weary to face any further stress and firmly stated: 'Too much water has passed under the bridge,' and walked away to collect my kit which had crossed London in another vehicle, only to find it had been stolen *en route*.

Boarding my train with no corridor I was promptly locked into an empty compartment by the guard. There was just me and my nylon stockings tucked under my tunic along with my small Bible and enclosures.

As I relaxed I soon became retrospective about strange involvements and the suffering when tortured till pain wearied itself into an anaesthetic, lulling me into sleeps of agony. I remembered the tangible glimpses of the Omnipotent which upheld me when on more than one occasion I stood face to face with dissolution. I know God is not mocked: 'for whatever a man soweth that also shall he reap'.

Without success I had tried to be 'an island' in a very hostile world, where man with his greed forgets we are on this blighted earth for a very short time; yet destruction seems to be his sole motivation. I did not recall passing Peterborough or Grantham, but the guard unlocked my compartment at Doncaster where I stretched my legs and scrounged a cup of tea. The only uniformed man on the train for Hull, I felt all my movements were being overshadowed.

In the darkness of a November night I arrived at Paragon Station in Hull. Not a porter was in sight at that hour. With my spare six and a half stone frame I fleetingly wondered what other entanglements of life were in store for me. Walking forward in the sombre light, the horizon was incredibly eerie. Every building in the vicinity had been razed to the ground, including my favourite Hammonds Emporium across from the Station. The shock turned my stomach over as I sought a hasty retreat from that vast demolition.

One lone 'Private Hire' car came into view, the only sign of life. Hopefully I asked, 'Could I cadge a lift to Cottingham?' The driver said 'I am not a registered hackney for fares in the station, but I saw you standing.' Reaching out hands to assist me we drove off into the night.

EPILOGUE

Fisher of Men, my catch is very little but that which I have is worth keeping.